Shad Roe

Published by BookLocker.com, Inc., Bradenton, FL.

Printed in the United States of America on acid-free paper.

BookLocker.com, Inc.
2014

First Edition

Acknowledgements

I remember when I started writing the first short story that would eventually become the basis for this book. It was an August evening. I had set up a computer on a card table in our bedroom. Our five children were all quite young at the time so the bedroom was the safest place for anything that we did not want to get broken. After a few nights of typing that had gone well past midnight, I became concerned that the noise of my fingers banging on the keyboard was keeping my wife from getting to sleep.

"It's fine," Barb assured me. "I like hearing you type." If she meant it or was just being polite, I wasn't sure. Nevertheless, her words gave me the encouragement I needed to keep writing—that night and in the years that followed. Barb, I cannot thank you enough.

There are many others who also helped me throughout this project—a project that sometimes became all-consuming. My children, Anna, Josh, Mary, Martha, and Sarah—all now grown, each provided me with more support than they will likely ever realize. I would be remiss if I did not also recognize those friends who encouraged me in my work, notably Nancy Cimprich in New Jersey and Mary Kathryn McIvor in Virginia. I am also deeply grateful to my colleagues at Neumann University in Aston, Pennsylvania, who contributed so much, among them: Dr. Janelle Ketrick-Gillespie, director of

Neumann University's Writing Program (who firmly believed that this was a story worth telling—a story that everyone could relate to, but no one was willing to talk about); Katie Callahan, for the hours spent proofreading and for her valuable feedback; and Bob Duffy, who—in addition to his hours of proofing—helped me discover the value of a metaphor as a title.

Without a doubt, though, the person who continued to give me the critical push I needed—sometimes hour by hour—to complete this book was Brian Wraight. Brian, a graduate of Northeastern University and the University of Denver's Publishing Institute, is a truly gifted editor. What he may lack in age is more than made up for in literary instinct and skill. The world is a better place because of his presence.

To all of you, my most sincere and heartfelt thanks.

James Randolph Jordan
West Chester, Pennsylvania
August 10, 2014

To Barb

Part One

I was in South Dakota. I had been there before. Long, winding, dirt and gravel roads rolling gently over treeless hills. My occasional trips were like those of others who made their living crisscrossing the country. But they were also different. Instead of bustling, traffic-bogged, big cities, my destinations were mostly small towns in the middle of nowhere— often little more than crossroads in a rural part of the world known for its extreme weather or for the part it played in a war a century ago.

Rather than working for a company, I worked for myself and working for myself always meant being cheap whenever I traveled. The cheapest flight, no matter what time it arrived. The cheapest hotel, no matter how saggy the beds were, and the cheapest rental car, even if everything about it wasn't working.

This time it was the air conditioner—it had stopped working somewhere around Pine Ridge, so I rolled down all of the car windows. It was noisy, windy, and hot.

When my phone rang, I slowed down—not wanting to take the chance of losing the call. In the midst of such outlands, cell phone signals were sketchy at best. Phone calls could come to an abrupt end.

"Hey," the voice said.

"Hey," I answered. It was my brother, Carter, and it was the way we always greeted one another—both on the phone and in person.

"They took Daddy to th' hospital this mornin'," he said. "He had another heart attack. They are sayin' he's only got about a thirty percent chance a' makin' it through th' night." I pulled over to the side of the road, stopped the car and held the phone closer to my ear. "They say if he does make it," my brother continued, "his chances'll improve. We'll jus' hafta wait 'n see."

"Awright," I answered. "Let me know if there's any change."

"I will."

"You awright?" I asked.

"Yeah . . . tired," he responded.

"Thanks for bein' there," I said.

"No problem." And with that, our phone call ended just as suddenly as it had begun.

I turned the car off and got out. I was surprised how quiet everything had suddenly become. There wasn't another car, building, or human being in sight—only a great expanse of barren hills and open fields. The vast stretches of wildflowers which had painted the landscape just a month earlier had now turned brown from the long summer sun. I took a deep breath and sighed, but before getting back into the car, I turned to take another look at the brown vastness that stretched to the horizon. I wished I could have seen the flowers.

Carter was my oldest brother. And even though our middle brother, Jack, and I had decided long ago that our lives would be better if we lived far away from Virginia—away from our parents and the pain of those relationships—Carter chose to live within half an hour's drive of our mother and father. With that decision, he became the responsible one—the one who would interact with our parents on birthdays, holidays, and special occasions, the one who would run the required errands and the one to tend to their needs as they aged.

When Mumma and Daddy were married in May, 1951, it wasn't exactly the wedding my grandmother had imagined for her daughter. Like all good Catholic mothers, Louise had prayed that her daughter—my mumma—would marry a man who would provide well, in fortune and in faith. Jackson, my father, did neither. The fact that Daddy had had his way with my mother prior to their wedding night—and that he had come to Highland Park by way of Church Hill—didn't sit well with my grandmother or any of Mumma's family. Most of my mother's brothers carried with them a hatred for my father to their dying day. And so there was a bit of discomfort at the union of Agnes and Jackson—from both sides of the family—he, white trash from Richmond's Church Hill neighborhood, and she, a pregnant mackerel-snapper. Nevertheless, it was better for my parents to have each other and their illusions than for her to be pregnant and unmarried, regardless of her faith or class. And seven months after their wedding, my oldest brother Carter was born.

When my brother Jack was born in 1953, my parents left Richmond and moved to Mechanicsville. The town was about a forty minute drive northeast of Richmond and, in those days, it was the picture of rural life—a gathering of small houses, a feed store, drug store, five and dime, gas station and a bar. Yet while it was just a short drive from the city, it seemed a world away from concrete sidewalks, traffic, and relatives.

My parents had moved to get away from their families. Daddy never wanted to be like his father—and Mumma would go wherever and whenever Daddy spoke. Whatever other reason the two of them had for getting out of Richmond, I'm not really sure—and in reality, I don't think it mattered much anyway. Whether we lived in rural Mechanicsville or in one of the old neighborhoods on Richmond's north side, the cards had been dealt a long time ago.

After about year in Mechanicsville, I came along. A little more than a year after that, my mother was pregnant with her fourth child. Each pregnancy and birth had been increasingly difficult for her. A distant relative had recently died during labor so the thought of dying during childbirth was not a far-fetched notion. When Jack was born, Mumma lost nearly half of her blood within a matter of a few minutes. In later years—whenever she spoke about those early years of our lives, she would remind whoever was around that Jack's delivery had almost killed her.

"I almost bled to death," Mumma would always say whenever she spoke about my middle brother. There seemed to be a thinly veiled indictment against my brother, as if she blamed him for all of the subsequent difficulties in her life. As she prepared for the birth of a fourth child, Mumma told Daddy that this was it. This was going to be the last pregnancy for her and after the baby had been delivered she would have her tubes tied. Daddy, a man of principle when he chose to be, vehemently opposed any kind of sterilization, finding such procedures not only unnatural, but also against the teachings of his somewhat-new-found Catholic faith. Nevertheless, Daddy agreed and—while my mother's womb was exposed during the Caesarean delivery, the doctor made sure my mother would never get pregnant again. As fate would have it, though, baby Rusty died within forty-eight hours and so for the remainder of his years—no matter how hard someone might have tried to convince him otherwise—Daddy firmly believed that a vengeful God took my younger brother. It was punishment for Daddy consenting to my mother's tubal ligation.

"God took that baby," my father would say matter-of-factly. It usually took about a half-bottle of Virginia Gentleman before he would bring it up. "It was ya mumma's goddamn fault. She shouldn'a signed those goddamn papers. I shouldn'a signed 'em either. Goddamn her!"

"No other reason for the baby to 've died—jus' no other reason," he would continue. "Don' make no sense. God did that. Shouldn'a signed those papers." Tears would be streaming down the old man's cheeks by the time those words would have come out. He would run his long sleeve across his nose. I learned early on not to say anything in response. It was better to just sit quiet.

"And then ya Big Mama," my father would continue, "she wanted to make sure I took the baby to Frank Bliley's new funeral home over on Grace Street—not Tom Bliley's. She kept saying that he was Catholic so I needed to support him. That he needed the business." Big Mama was my maternal grandmother.

"Damnedest thing for her to be thinkin' about somebody gettin' business while my baby was dead and ya mumma was still in th' hospital." In a lot of ways, for the rest of his life, whatever had caused my brother's death remained secondary to Daddy. After all, crib death—as it was called back then—wasn't that unusual. Instead, what haunted him most was not only the fact that he and my mother had done something to cause a vengeful God to rob them of their child, but that the world, the family, and the life he had hoped for were gone.

My parents' marriage lasted for almost twenty years, at least on paper. The nearly two decades they were together and raising three boys were anything but happy or blissful. Both of our parents—"Mumma" and "Daddy" as most children we knew addressed their parents—were themselves children of alcoholic fathers . . . men who had abused their wives as well as the boys or girls they produced.

There are few words to describe my father's childhood other than miserably poor. Even though his family lived in the city, as late as 1948, they still only had cold running water. They also used an outhouse instead of an indoor toilet. My daddy's father, Big Papa, worked as a handy man and house painter and usually drank away what little take-home pay he earned. Childhood diseases ravaged poor and wealthy families alike in those days. My daddy and his siblings, though, got more than their share. In 1931, when my father was three, he and his older sister, Connie, who was five, both contracted polio. Neither of them came through it unscathed. As Daddy got older, his right leg became shorter than his left—causing him to develop a limp which got worse throughout his life. Connie spent her life with her legs supported by metal braces. My aunt Lois, Daddy's younger sister, caught a childhood infection which left her blind in one eye and my father's youngest sister, Ruth, came down with scarlet fever which left her completely deaf. In the early 1940s, Tommy, Daddy's youngest brother, died from measles.

"Tommy died in the bedroom upstairs in our house on Twenty-Third Street," my father once explained when he had drunk more than he needed. "My daddy—ya Big Papa—wasn't home when it happened so ya Nanny told me to go find him . . . ta tell him that Tommy was dead. I walked around half 'a Church Hill lookin' fa that man. When I finally found him, he was with some woman. He was all dressed up, lookin' like he was on a date." Daddy stopped speaking, lost in his thoughts.

"When I found him, he was standing with this woman in front of a house. When he saw me comin' towards him, he said, 'Hey boy, whadya doin' here?'

"I told him, 'Mumma sent me. Tommy's dead.'

"He just looked at me and asked me if there was anything else. I shook my head. 'Awright,' he said. Jus' like that. Then he told me to go on back home."

The scars my father bore weren't limited to his mind or his shortened leg. In the center of Daddy's left cheek was a deep mark—about an inch long—that created the illusion of a hole in his face. On more than one occasion, Mumma explained how Daddy got his scars.

"Big Papa was a mean, spiteful man," my mother would begin with each telling of the story. "That man beat ya Nanny and ya father whenever and wherever he felt like it. He would'a beat me if I had stayed around their house long enough. Why ya Nanny ever stayed with him is beyond me."

Nanny was the affectionate name we had given to my daddy's mumma. She was a large woman, big-boned, handsome, almost as tall as our father, but kindness and gentleness were what I recall most about her. She had a gentle spirit that loved most of God's creatures and tolerated Catholics.

"One night—when ya daddy and I were still dating—ya grandfather came home drunk. Ya daddy was only about eighteen." At this point, my mother wandered for a moment, lost in the mist of reminiscence.

"Anyway," she continued, "ya grandfather started beatin' on ya Nanny—smacking her, hitting her, pulling her hair, calling her all kinds 'a names. Ya daddy got between Nanny and ya grandfather . . . holding Big Papa's arms down so he couldn't hit Nanny. Well, eventually, Big Papa got the upper hand and started beating Jackson." Retelling the story, my mother seemed to forget that it was my father she was speaking about—often referring to him by name. "Ya grandfather had this big ring he wore on his right hand and that ring punched a hole in ya daddy's cheek. I saw ya daddy the next day and he had about half a dozen stitches in his cheek from where he'd been hit."

"About a week or two later," Mumma continued, "Big Papa came home again—drunk—mean as a snake. He started beating on ya Nanny again. This time when ya daddy tried to stop him again, Big Papa punched Jackson over and over again in the face, aiming for the spot where he had been cut the first time. After a few punches, the old cut opened again, worse than before. There was blood everywhere. Ya daddy went to the hospital, but his face was really torn up. That scar never really healed right."

When my parents met at George Bruce's horse farm near Cold Harbor, my father had already converted to Catholicism. A few years before, Daddy had fallen in love with another Richmond girl who was Catholic—which was a highly unimaginable thing since there was only about one Catholic for every five thousand Baptists. He had converted to Catholicism in the back room of a rectory so as to be able to marry the girl. For some reason, though, the relationship didn't last. Nevertheless, long after Mumma and Daddy were married, my father kept tucked in his wallet a tattered, yellowing photograph of a young woman standing beside a black Ford—a pretty girl with long, wavy, black hair, wearing a tight sweater and a flowing skirt.

A few years before he died, during one of my visits with my father at his house in Richmond, we had spent a couple of hours talking. It was more rambling than talking. Politics, the weather, whatever. As usual, though, our conversation always returned to the past.

"I went to the cemetery on my way over," I said. "I saw Connie's grave, then I started looking for Nanny's grave and ya daddy's . . . took a while, but I finally found them. She died when I was in college, but I don't really remember him much."

"I got a picture of him," Daddy said from the stuffed chair across the room. He reached for his wallet, moving like the old man he had become. "That's him when I was a kid—around '36 or '37 . . . I think. It's written on the back somewhere." He handed me the small photo. "What's it say?"

"Yeah, Easter 1937."

"That was taken in Chimborazo Park. I remember that picture being taken. You can have that."

"Thanks, Daddy."

I noticed he had thumbed through a number of photos before offering me the one of his father. Curiosity was getting the best of me.

"What's that other picture you got?"

He sat for a moment, glancing at me, then back to the image in his hand, then back to me. Finally, after a few seconds, he stretched out his hand laying the old snap gently in mine.

"Pretty," I said. "Who is she?"

"Somebody I knew a long time ago," my father answered. "Before ya mumma."

I didn't ask him if he loved her, or if he had been intimate with her. That wasn't any of my business, nor would it have been proper for a son to ask such things of a parent. I knew my father had been with a lot of women throughout the years—before, during, and after his marriage to my mother. Along with the Easter Bunny, Santa Claus, and the Tooth Fairy, I had given up any illusions of my father's purity and fidelity a long time ago.

"What happened?" I asked.

"Wha' ya mean?"

"What happened to her?"

"It jus' didn't work out." As I continued staring at the picture, my father sat in silence. "I wanted to marry her," he continued after a moment. "That's when I became Catholic . . . in the rectory at St. Patrick's on Church Hill. But then it didn't happen. She broke my heart." My father had told me more than I ever could have imagined he would. Without a word, I handed the photo back to him. I didn't press any further.

By the late 1950s, Daddy had become that which he had sworn he never would be—a violent, raging alcoholic with an uncontrollable temper who often directed his vicious anger towards those he loved most. In too many ways, he had become his father. Accompanying the violence were the trysts that developed as a result of his insatiable appetite for illicit sex and a job that gave him the open road for an office. After only a few years of marriage, the combination was taking its toll on our family—and by 1965, our parents' marriage was quickly deteriorating.

Around the same time, one of my father's indiscretions—a teenage girl from the backwoods of Virginia—became pregnant. Without divorcing my mumma, Daddy set up a second household and started a second family in a small rural farming community just west of Fredericksburg. Just as his father had managed two wives and two sets of children in two distinct households back in the 1930s, Daddy decided to try doing the same. The trouble was, our father had a hard enough time managing one family, so two wouldn't last very long. My parents' marriage came to an end.

It was a horrible time for all of us. Daddy had chosen his "other family" over ours. Some weekends we saw him. Others, we didn't. My brothers and I believed that the time would come when things would eventually get better—that our father would return to us and life would once again offer us some type of normalcy. But in midsummer of 1967, Daddy collected all of his belongings and moved out.

Divorce is never an easy, quick or simple thing. In my adult years, whenever I have spoken about my childhood with a therapist or some other mental health professional, they inevitably use the term "broken home." But "broken" always seemed like a term better saved for describing pieces of china scattered on a kitchen floor. Divorce, especially when children are involved, is a lot messier than that.

The thing most children hold dearest to them is their family. It is the child's source of who they are—their identity. When I was eight years old, if you asked me who I was, I would have told you my name, the names of my brothers, who my parents were and where my house was. For a child, those individual relationships form a single entity. That single thing is the source of security, the source of love and grace—the grace that gives a child the knowledge that there is a unique, blood-bond between these people.

Now, imagine that the family is gone, I would explain. Unlike something that is broken, it cannot be mended or put back together again. As a child, you have no idea what is going to happen to you. Your world—the world as you know it—is suddenly gone. Forever. Once divorce occurs, a person can no longer say, "I am going to stay with my family." They can only say I am going to stay with my brother or sister or mother or father. The family is gone.

As we grew older, my brothers and I each found our own way of grieving the passing of our family. Carter, who would always be seen as the most successful of the three of us, chose to immerse himself in his job, working fourteen and fifteen hour days, year after year. Those things most substantial in his life were nearly all associated with his career or the assortment of professional organizations and clubs to which he belonged. Jack, like our oldest brother, also found himself "immersed" in things throughout his life. His addictions, though, were much less acceptable in the public's eye. Jack dropped out of high school and joined the Navy when he was seventeen. During his late teens, he began to use cocaine. As he grew older, he also became an alcoholic. Sex became an addiction as well. And after three failed marriages, he struggled just to function.

For my part, I also have my share of addictions and issues. Instead of work, cocaine, drugs or alcohol, my drug of choice has been food. I eat to soothe whatever is gnawing at me. Like my oldest brother, I belong to my share of social clubs—usually with names like Weight Watchers, Overeaters Anonymous and Jenny Craig. At some hours of the day, anything that is not nailed down is fair game for consumption.

Like any addiction, it has also wreaked havoc on my health and my relationships. It threatens to consume me every day. Unlike my brothers, though, for me God became as big a part of my life as food. After high school, I first attended a seminary, then a number of colleges and universities searching desperately for some way to make sense of all that we had endured. Eventually, I was appointed pastor of a church—believing that my interaction with the faithful would also serve as a source of enlightenment in my darkness. Throughout my life, though—even as I preached on Sundays—I often wondered where God was in those years so long ago. I wondered where his love and protection were every time my father flew into a rage. I wondered where God's peace was when my father terrified his children. I wondered where justice was when my father beat a helpless son or daughter. And when it came time for my father to die, I wondered where God would be on that day of reckoning. Would anyone know everything he had done? Would it be like it is written in the Bible—where everything secret is shouted from the rooftops? *Jesus, I hoped not.*

Part Two

As the hours passed without hearing from Carter again, I realized that, just as he had numerous times during the past twenty years, Daddy had made it through another health crisis. In many ways, our father's health and his uncanny ability to cheat death had become a recurring joke. Years of alcoholism and a five-pack-a-day cigarette habit had taken their toll on his heart, lungs, and nearly every other organ. Over the course of two decades, my father had survived at least three strokes, seven heart attacks and an aneurism in his aorta. Somehow, though, he always managed to return to the land of the living, cursing death and perhaps a doctor or nurse who might be in the same room.

More than a day had passed since Carter and I had first spoken. I was home when the phone rang again.

"Hey," the voice said on the other end of the telephone. It was Carter. "Well, things were lookin' up til this mornin'," he said with a bit more emotion than his voice usually revealed. "About three hours ago, though, he began goin' downhill. He's been hooked up to a ventilator and an automatic defibrillator since he was admitted, but the doctors are now sayin' we should disconnect 'im . . . that his heart is jus' too weak to recover. He's just existin' right now." He stopped speaking for a few seconds, then continued. "So that's what we're gonna do." There was silence.

"Okay," I said. Beneath our conversation I was still trying to listen for something unsaid, something unspoken—to determine if Carter was overreacting in some way, if this really was going to be the end of my father's life.

"Just wanted to let you know," he concluded.

Like all of our conversations, this one ended quickly. As I hung up the phone, I sat thinking about my father, but not too much. For years, I had wondered how I would respond to his death, wondering what kind of thoughts would enter my mind when the man who had abused my brothers and me in ways too terrible to describe was finally gone. So before I began considering too seriously that my father might really be dying, I wanted to make sure it was actually going to happen. Whatever the mental struggle or anguish was going to be, I didn't want to go through it prematurely. I didn't want to start down that road until I was sure it was time.

I lay in bed thinking about what was happening in my father's hospital room more than three hundred miles away. It was a mid-August night, hot, without a stirring breeze or the slightest whisper of a distant wind. As the hours passed, I recalled other nights in my life—from my childhood long ago—when I had thought about life and death and my father.

One thing I've learned throughout my adult life is that memories never come in any particular order. They don't come like they happened. I'd be lying if I said they did. I think anyone would. Instead, memory is a fickle thing . . . almost as if it has a mind of its own, coming and going as it pleases—twisting itself, reinterpreting itself, reimagining itself—all according to its own desire. We don't think of things from our early childhood and then our late childhood, followed by our teen years and so on. Thoughts just come—like uninvited neighbors to an impromptu cookout. And just like those unwelcome guests, memories— especially the unpleasant ones—stay much longer than we want them to. They linger, strolling around inside the head, making comments about this or that, making a mess of the thoughts which just moments before had been so organized. I used to try telling them to leave, but it never worked. They always stay until they are done doing whatever it is they have come to do. Lately, I've begun to compare them not only to "unwelcome guests," but to the unwelcome guests who have had too much to drink. You never know what is going to set them off.

Anything can trigger a memory. Sure, pictures are obvious triggers. Photographs are to memories like flashing lights are to police cars. If you see one, you know the other is coming. For me, though, it's the less obvious triggers that bring the memories or recollections which bring the most havoc. Recollections triggered by a hint of a smell, a wisp of wind blowing a certain direction, or a slight sound—like cicadas on a summer evening.

Throughout the days and nights that followed Carter's phone call, those unwelcome guests kept coming, staying much longer than I wanted them to. There were the simple, small ones. Then the big ones. Ones that always involved my daddy. Ones that involved life changing events. And as usual, they created havoc. They always do.

No matter what time of year it was—fall, winter, spring or summer—my brothers and I always had to be in bed by 7:00. Even though daylight savings time had already had plenty of time to kick in—and the summer sun was still pretty high—the Jordan boys were in bed and lights out by 7:00. Of course the lights were always out by 7:00 because it was still so sunny outside that no one needed their lights on anyway.

Our bedroom was small. Carter's bed was against one wall and Jack and I shared bunk beds against the other wall. There was little room between the three beds—so little that Jack could easily jump from his top bunk across the room and onto Carter, which he often did, without ever having to touch the floor. But this night—after our baths and kissing our parents goodnight—we settled down with the windows cranked open, longing for any hint of a breeze that would cool our room.

As we lay in our beds, we could hear Buck and Gladys Perkins starting to argue from the house next door. The summer heat not only meant that we listened for a breeze making its way into our room, but on a regular basis, we also listened for Buck to come home and begin his drunken tirade. My brothers and I would laugh quietly at the words that came from the house next door—words that we were forbidden to say—but it sure was entertaining to hear them from our neighbor's mouth. For a short while, we wondered what kinds of obscenities Buck would say next, but then our laughter slowly faded, Daddy had already finished off a six pack of Schlitz before we had even gotten into bed.

Even as a child, I knew my daddy was a man filled with rage. He hated his own father who had beaten both him and his mother. He was angry at those who had said he wasn't good enough to be the husband of their daughter and sister. He was angry at those who said he wasn't good enough to be the father of their grandchildren. He was angry at a mother who said that he was too much like his father. And this night, he brought that anger home to my mother, my brothers, and me.

It was the middle of the night—around three o'clock in the morning I later figured. That's what the clock in the kitchen said when it was all over, after everything quieted down.

"What's wrong?" I asked waking up from a deep sleep.

"Shhhh!" Carter whispered. "Mumma 'n Daddy are fightin'."

Woven throughout our conversation were the sounds of dishes breaking and my parents screaming at one another. All I could make out were a lot of goddamns and shits being slurred by my father. My mother was pleading for him to stop. After a few minutes, the sound of crashing dishes ended. Clumsy footsteps crunched across a floor of broken glass. Heavy, heaving sobs now came from the living room. Carter, Jack, and I climbed out of our beds and looked out from the doorway of our room. We stared into the living room where the deep cries and heaves had been the loudest. There, my father lay collapsed in a heap on the vinyl couch. With each breath his body heaved up and down. His greasy black hair was tousled and strewn across his head. As he turned to look at us, his face glimmered from a mixture of snot and saliva smeared across his cheeks and chin. My mother saw us looking through the doorway and quietly beckoned us to come into the living room.

"Tell ya daddy you love him, boys," she said with

tears streaming down her cheeks. The look on her face filled me with fear and pity. "Go on," she continued, "give him a kiss 'n tell him you love him." We looked at my mother to see if there was any hint of insincerity or mockery—but there wasn't. She only stared at our father with an empty, mindless gaze. She stood just a few feet away from us—in limbo—in the doorway between the living room and kitchen. Behind her, we could see the kitchen floor. There lay what must have been a thousand pieces of broken china. Fine fragments of dinner plates, dessert plates, cups and saucers—a wedding gift from a family friend long ago—now carpeted the floor. What had moments ago been the only beautiful thing my mother ever owned was now nothing more than tiny bits and shards of glass.

As I walked over and kissed my father lightly on the forehead, he reached up and grabbed my arm. I stood terrified—unable to move. Pee ran down my leg. The powerful hands that had smashed dishes and punched through plaster walls now held me. He pulled my shoulders and head close to his. I looked at my mother and wondered if she would do something or say something to rescue me, but she just smiled a sickly smile. Daddy pressed his glistening face against mine. His snot and spit were now smeared on both of us.

"I love you, Ran," he slurred as he kissed me. The smell of whiskey and vomit blew onto my face. As he let me go, I backed away and stood behind Carter as he, too, cried.

"Ya daddy loves you boys," my mother said, still managing a vacant smile. Jack stood there still sobbing—wiping his face with his hands. "Y'all go on back to bed now," she said. None of us answered her.

In the weeks that followed—as the days and nights got hotter—it became our duty not to talk about that thing that had happened. Not to say anything to our friends, or each other. My mother never spoke about it. On more than one occasion, though, as I came into the kitchen, I would see her wistfully standing there looking at the empty shelves that hung on the walls beneath the cabinets. Standing there, staring at the bare wood, she wouldn't say a word. She would just stand there and stare. No one said a word about the events of that night.

As the sun began heating up the day, there was still no word from my oldest brother. My thoughts returned to my father lying in a hospital bed. More than a few times, I laughed thinking I had almost been duped into too hastily contemplating my father's death. At least once every other year for the past fifteen years, I had received a phone call from Carter telling me that Daddy was in the hospital having suffered another heart attack or stroke and that the doctors had said that our father might not make it through the night. The old man was beating the odds once again, I thought. Whoever said, "Only the good die young," certainly knew what they were talking about. I convinced myself to give it one more day and my brother would be calling to tell me Daddy was sitting up and eating a breakfast of scrambled eggs—making suggestive remarks to a pretty young nurse. Daddy loved scrambled eggs.

Fish eggs, or to be more specific, shad roe, was something I learned to identify early in my life. A body always had to look hard at what my mother was fixing for a meal—especially when Daddy wasn't around. I didn't know whether it was from her upbringing or something she had heard in passing conversation, but Mumma held strongly to the notion that children had to be fed things that didn't taste good, because things that didn't taste good must be good for you. As a matter of principle, the worse something tasted, the better it was for you.

Mumma slid a plate of scrambled eggs in front of each of us and told us to say grace. After the "Amen"—Carter, Jack, and I each grabbed a piece of toast from the plate in the middle of the table and began chewing. Our kitchen was small. Actually, our whole house was small. There were two bedrooms, a bathroom, living room and kitchen. My mother said we had a pantry, but none of us ever really quite knew exactly where it was. There were a few shelves behind the back door that led out of the kitchen and into the back yard. She would keep cans of food, a box of powdered milk and empty paper bags there. Next to the shelves, sitting on the floor, was a twenty-five pound bag of dog chow. We figured that was the pantry.

The kitchen itself was dark yellow. A neighbor friend of my mother's called it "duck-shit yellow." The walls were dark yellow. The chairs had dark, yellow vinyl seats with yellow vinyl backs with chrome legs. The table, with its yellow and gray Formica top and chrome legs, matched the chairs. Even the phone that hung on the wall with its long curly cord was yellow. And on this particular morning, the color of the scrambled eggs matched the rest of the kitchen.

"The eggs look funny," I said to my mother. Carter and Jack had already started on theirs, but not without drinking large amounts of powdered milk and eating a few pieces of toast between each forkful.

"Just eat 'em, Randy," she answered. "How many children in Africa do you think would love to have 'em?"

I wasn't sure where Africa was or what kind of eggs they had there, but I was contemplating making a swap. As I took the first bite, I chewed carefully—not wanting to be too surprised at whatever was coming. "They taste funny," I said. "Kind 'a fishy." At that point I realized what had happened. My mother had mixed large amounts of shad roe in with a few scrambled eggs. My brothers had fought this battle too many times and lost. It appeared that this time they surrendered without even a word. I, on the other hand, wasn't about to go down so easily.

"Mumma, what's in the eggs?" I whined.

"It's shad roe," she shot back.

"What's roe?" I asked. She snickered a little, but Carter, Jack, and I didn't see anything to laugh about.

"They're fish eggs," Carter said. "Jus' eat 'em."

"They'll make you smart," my mother explained.

"I don't want 'em," I whined again. "Can I just have some plain eggs?"

"You boys go on out 'n play," Mumma said to my brothers as they sat there watching me gag. "You finish your breakfast," Mumma said pointing at me, "before I give you something to really whine about."

I choked down the rest of the shad roe while Carter and Jack ran out the back door and off to play with friends. By the time I had finished, they were long gone. It was better that way for them. Rarely did they want their little brother tagging along in the building of forts or in the BB gun fights that were so much a part of their lives.

I went out the back door and walked a short distance down the gravel road towards Brent MacDougall's. His was a small, white stucco ranch-style home. The design of the house always seemed odd to me—never quite fitting in with the tiny cement block houses that everyone else had. The MacDougall's also had more property than the rest of us. Next to their house were a couple of acres where they grew their own vegetables—mostly potatoes, tomatoes, watermelons and some pole beans. Each summer, as each crop ripened at its appointed time, Brent and I would sit under a small tree and sample the first-fruits of the season. With no water nearby to wash the vegetables, each of us consumed more than our share of dirt with each bite.

The time in the garden made for the most pleasant memories of the summer—that and catching animals. Guarded by an assortment of oaks, maples and pines that stood at the crest of a small rise just above where the tomatoes were planted, we sat there in the weeds beneath a shady tree, biting into the ripest tomatoes we could find. At almost twelve years old, Brent amazed me with his knowledge of wild things like squirrels and rabbits and such. In the years I had known him—which had pretty much been all my life—he had taught me just about everything I knew about finding animals that might be hiding somewhere. And if he didn't know it, we would go ask his Grandma, a slight old woman with a sun bonnet and gingham dress who always came to stay with Brent's mumma and daddy, Ora and Davis, during the summer months. But this time, Brent didn't need to ask Grandma MacDougall.

"I was at th' pond yestaday," Brent said. He took another bite of a tomato. "I saw a turtle I know was at least two feet across."

"Uh, uh," I protested.

"Uh, huh," he shot back. "I'll bet if we went there right now, I could find it."

"If ya don't, you owe me a Pepsi-Cola," I said.

"Awright."

As we made our way out of the field, we followed a narrow dirt path that would take us to the edge of Old Man Gagnon's pond. On one side of the path was a marshy piece of land that was filled with loud crickets and a few noisy frogs. On the other side was a slow, stagnant creek filled with brackish water and mosquitoes. It wasn't the kind of place where a kid would play—especially during the hot summer when the water put off such an awful foul smell.

As we began to wander further down the path, we both noticed a large, dark object slowly making its way across the dirt just a few yards in front of us. It was a snapping turtle! Just as I had secretly hoped he would be, Brent was right.

While some of the snapping turtles in the creeks nearby were just of medium size, the overwhelming majority of them were huge. Of course these were the only snapping turtles I had ever really seen. But Brent once told me that Old Man Gagnon—who he said had produced most of the turtles in Virginia—fed them dead snakes and rotten fish which made them not only extra big, but mean as well. And if Brent told me, then it had to be true.

The biggest ones were a solid dark green with a high bumpy ridge that ran straight down the middle of the shell on their backs. Their legs weren't as stumpy as most other turtles. Even though they were covered with scales as with a suit of mighty armor, they could move quite quickly on dry ground. The claws on their feet were long and sharp and could tear a man to pieces—at least that's what I was told. Their mouth had a shape like a dinosaur's head with a hook-shaped beak at the end. The worst part of all, though, was that—according to legend—if a body ever got bitten by a snapper, it wouldn't let go of you until there was thunder. Neither my brothers nor I, nor any other kids I knew had ever seen a person get bitten by a snapper—so we didn't know if the legend was true. But at the same time, none of us was ever going to put it to the test.

Brent and I started yelling and jumping as soon as we saw the huge turtle. It had to be at least two feet across and must have weighed a good twenty five pounds. The sheer size of this beast meant that we couldn't keep this treasure to ourselves. No one would believe us if we just told them about it. They would have to see it for themselves.

As carefully as he could, Brent reached under the turtle's shell and flipped it over on its back. "You grab the legs," he said pointing to the front claws.

"I ain't grabbin' those things!" I answered. "It'll rip me to pieces!" I said. I remembered Brent's warning to me from a long while ago.

"Okay then," he said, "I'll get the front and you get the back!" The turtle had stretched out its claws, moving them as fast as it could in the air, desperately trying to right itself. At the same time, it was making loud breathing noises—pushing air out of its lungs—trying to scare us. It was working.

"Hurry up," Brent said, "get it before it gets right side up!"

"I'll grab the tail," I answered.

While Brent was carefully grabbing the front claws, I took hold of the spiky tail. As we started to lift it off the ground, I didn't like the feel of the thing, so I dropped it.

"Wait a minute," I said. Pulling at the bottom of my tee shirt, I stretched it as far as I could to make a glove so as to once again grab the spiky, green tail. Together Brent and I lifted the snapper and began carrying it back up the path and onto the gravel road we had traveled just a few minutes before. As we did, the turtle continued to stretch its head out as far as it could, all the while trying to snap its jaws down on any of Brent's fingers. Finally, as we struggled to haul it up the hill towards our homes, we decided that we had carried it far enough.

"Let's drop it when we get to the top of the hill," Brent said. And after only a few more steps, with just a look toward each other, we let the giant snapper fall squarely on its stomach.

"Go get your brothers!" Brent told me. "I'll make sure it doesn't get away!"

Within minutes I was back with Carter and Jack. By that time, Little Tom showed up—a boy who shared the same name as my brother, Jack, but was a lot smaller. We never wanted to confuse the two boys who had the same name, so we changed the smaller Jack's name (the one who was not my brother) to Little Tom. The kid didn't mind and for all practical purposes, it seemed to work. So that was it. Little Tom lived across the creek and up a hill and had been heading up to visit Brent's cousin, Wayne. The five of us stood there gawking at the magnificent turtle. We all took turns giving it a kick or a poke as each of us asked the question of what to do with the thing.

"We could take it over to Gagnon's pond," Little Tom said.

"Naw," the rest of us objected. Within a moment our pokes had turned to jabs with sticks we had fetched. Somebody had even started to stand on the turtle to see how much weight the poor creature could hold before the shell caved in. Finally, Brent pulled his hatchet from its sheath and began to tap lightly on the top of the turtle's back.

"We could take it to my Grandma 'n she could make turtle soup!" Brent said.

Silently we stood for a moment—looking at one another for approval. We knew that if we did decide to take it to Grandma MacDougall, it wouldn't get there alive.

Within a moment of the declaration that the turtle's fate was soup, each of us launched a series of blows and kicks so severe that no one—not even a human—could have withstood the punishment. Sharpened sticks became spears and rusty coat hangers became instruments to dig beneath the scales that protected the reptile. Finally, Brent took the hatchet and gave the first awful, destructive blow. We all stood stunned at first, amazed at the gash that the sharp, metal blade had made in the creature's protective armor. But we were not to be content with only one whack of the hatchet. Soon we all began taking turns as we wielded blow upon blow. First a front leg was chopped off just below the shell. Blood and dark ooze started to flow wildly out of what was now the stub of a leg. Jack and Little Tom each took a turn hacking into the large shell that covered the creature's back. Carter took a chop at it without much success.

"Look how thick 'n hard that thing is," someone shouted in the excitement.

We were like a pack of wild dogs ripping and tearing at the carcass of a helpless deer. Our voices became shrieks of hysterical laughter as our hands and arms jerked and pulled at the creature. Our feet danced with the excitement of the kill. Finally, I asked for my turn. In the heat of the frenzy, I kicked the turtle over on its back and began hacking away into its underbelly. Blood, pieces of shell and soft turtle meat spewed into the air around us with each thwack of the hatchet. And within a moment, the turtle was dead.

Slowly, each boy left and gradually returned to the thing from which he had been called away. Brent picked up the turtle by the edges of the cracked and blood-covered shell and threw the carcass into a nearby ditch. During the next few days, whenever we walked near the spot where Brent had discarded the remains, we would smell the rotting flesh. But none of us said anything about it or even mentioned it in passing. And just as my brothers and I never spoke about the things that had happened in our house, Brent never spoke about the whippings he received from his daddy. We didn't speak about the turtle or any of the other horrible things we did, nor did we speak about the drunken rages or beatings or lashings that were also a part of our lives. Certain things were destined to remain secret. Instead, we spoke about the things we held dear, like sitting in the garden on a hot summer day. It was just better that way.

Part Three

As the day grew on, my thoughts turned from one memory of my father to another. While many of the memories that filled my thoughts that day were unpleasant to say the least, it would be unfair to say that I have no good memories of my father. There were times when my father could be gentle and loving—even overwhelming with his mercy. Both of my brothers had at some point shared with me one story of Daddy's kindness—times when his love had reflected that of something more sublime. For Carter, his fond recollections were created over a few years. Jack's over a few seasons. Mine happened in an afternoon.

In June 1965, I was just completing the fourth grade at St. Elizabeth's School in Highland Park. Even though it was a small school, it had a bus that made the drive out to Mechanicsville every morning to pick up the Catholic kids there, about ten or twelve in all. There was just one school day left before the start of summer vacation. As I left for school that morning, my mother told me that instead of riding the bus home, I was to walk to my grandmother's when the two-thirty bell rang. Big Mama, my mother's mother, lived only two blocks from the school and going there usually meant I would be sitting with her, eating red Jello in a bowl of skim milk by three o'clock, and then watching Sailor Bob on TV. This particular afternoon, though, my cousin Albert would be at Big Mama's as well. Perhaps we would be able to find something to do, my mother reminded me that morning, instead of watching television.

Albert was my mother's brother's son and, even though he was just a few months older than me, he was already in the fifth grade—but at a different school. After we finished our Jello and milk, Albert and I decided to join a group of public school kids— "publicans" as they came to be called by our family— for a neighborhood game of hide-and-seek. Whenever I had been at Big Mama's, I had never been allowed to play with the publicans. These children were, after all, living on Third Avenue, not Second, so they were bordering on being white trash—because the kids on Fourth Avenue were beyond help. It was best that I not spend time with them, my mother would tell me.

But on this day, Mumma was not around and Albert was with me. So, I decided, hanging out with these other kids would be okay because my cousin could easily shield me from any bad influence.

While an older boy hid his face against a tree, the rest of us—about eight in all—made our way through the maze of houses within the block searching for the best place to hide.

"Twenty-one, twenty-two, twenty-three . . . ," the boy counted. Looking around, I saw the perfect spot—a large bush bursting with so many leaves it could easily consume me. As I pushed my way from the back of the bush into its center, I felt another body already crouched and sitting low in the middle of the greenery. It was Albert.

"This's my spot," he said, emphasizing his claim.

"There ain't enough time for me to find another spot," I answered as the seeker began to shout more loudly.

"Forty-six, forty-seven, forty-eight . . . ."

"Besides, it's big 'nough for the both of us."

"Awright," my cousin said. "Git low 'n be quiet."

The publicans never did find us that afternoon. After nearly half an hour of seeking, the older kid gave up and called for us to come out. As Albert and I climbed out from the big bush, the game came to an end. We could also hear Big Mama calling for us from the back porch of her house just across the alley. It had been a fun afternoon. After dinner, Mumma arrived to take me home.

The next morning was Saturday so we usually slept until eight or so. When I finally climbed out of bed, I noticed that my face felt "heavy"—that was the only word I knew to describe it. It felt big, swollen, itchy and hot. I went into the bathroom to look in the mirror and what looked back at me was enough to scare me to tears.

"Mumma!"

"What's wrong?" my mother answered from the kitchen.

"I dunno!"

"Whadya mean?" At that point my mother now stood at the bathroom door. Looking at me, she gasped. "Good Lawd!"

As the day grew older, my face grew bigger. Tiny blisters had begun to appear. My ears, too, were turning bright red and puffy. By Sunday, I looked like the scariest villain any comic book artist could ever have hoped to create. Every inch of my face as well as my nose and lips were swollen, beet-red and covered with tiny, oozing blisters. My fingers had begun to swell and my ears now looked like those of a professional boxer, curled and twice their normal size. My cousin Albert, I was told, was suffering with a similar condition. Upon investigation by my uncle, it was evident that the best hiding place Albert and I had found during our game of hide-and-seek the day before was in the center of a poison sumac bush. We were suffering the consequences of playing with the publicans.

On Monday, Mumma took me to see Doctor Mikaelian. The Mikaelians had come to Richmond sometime in the first half of the twentieth century along with a host of other Armenian refugees. Many of them had settled in Church Hill. Like my daddy's family, they were poor. I suppose that's the main reason why Daddy found so much in common with the immigrant children he hung out with during his teenage years. They were outcasts looking for a place where people did not hate them or mistreat them. So was he. Daddy had become such good friends with one Armenian boy, a fellow by the name of Frank Derderian, that—rather than asking his brother Jimmy to be his best man, Daddy asked Frank. Even our dentist, Dr. Ghazarian, was Armenian.

Doctor Mikaelian was a small man with black, greasy hair that was brushed back and to the side. His broad smile revealed a mouthful of teeth that had not seen a dentist in a very long while.

"These pills he can take," he said shaking his head while looking at me. As he began writing the prescription, he reached in the bottom drawer of his desk.

For a short moment, I grew excited. "He's gonna give me some pills right now!" I thought. But as his hand drew back from the drawer, he threw a small amount of peanuts into his mouth. He had recently given up smoking and had discovered that peanuts were a decent substitute for tobacco. He handed my mother the prescription.

As he looked at me, he shook his head and laughed. My mother joined him in laughter, all the while repelled at the sight standing before her. Pink, cracked and flaking pieces of dried calamine now covered my hands, face, and ears. The lotion had done nothing to provide relief from the continuous itching and only seemed to make my appearance all the more terrifying.

"Mumma," I said with tears now oozing from my eyes, "help me."

Even though the doctor assured her I wasn't contagious, my mother refused to touch me. She could not see past the yellow, now-crusty, blisters oozing from my face.

After the visit to the doctor, Mumma took me to Nanny's house—a long, narrow duplex located on a side street in Richmond's west end. After Big Papa died in 1963, Nanny lived alone. To support herself, she worked as the manager of an ice cream shop, which meant that if we ever came to visit her, we would get free ice cream. My parents, though, rarely took her up on the invitation. Each morning, Nanny would walk a half-block from her house and catch the number four bus that would take her to work. Late every evening, she would make the trip back home— and repeat the routine six days a week. This day, though, she had taken time off to be at home while my father painted her kitchen.

Ashamed and embarrassed, I sat crying in the back seat of the car—covering my face with blistered, swollen hands. I didn't want to get out.

"Come in here," my mother demanded.

As we walked through the front door, Mumma called to Daddy who was there painting Nanny's kitchen.

"Back here," my father responded.

As we walked down the hallway towards the back of the house, my crying grew more intense at the thought of what my father and grandmother would say. I wanted to die.

"Look at him," my mother said laughing as we entered the kitchen.

For a quick instant, Daddy sat silently looking at me. Then, in the most gentle of gestures, he became that which all fathers are created to be. Smiling softly, he looked at my swollen face—eyes now crusted over, oozing and weeping. "Come here, boy," he said—and with that, he stretched out his arms, wrapped them around me and held me close to his chest. In all my life, for all my days, for every moment of which I had existed, I had never cherished anything more than his embrace that afternoon. I would remember that moment for the rest of my life. There would come a time when I thought he would hold me again like that—loving, caring, protecting me. But I was wrong. Daddy was always looking for a little more.

Part Four

It was two-thirty in the afternoon when Carter did finally call again. And once more, the conversation was short.

"He's gone."

"What?"

"Daddy's gone . . . about ten minutes ago."

I sat with the phone pressed hard against the side of my head, not sure what to say. I tried to speak, to say something, to make some noise, but I couldn't.

"You there?" he asked.

I tried harder to say anything. My response finally came as a whisper creeping up from the back of my throat. "Thanks. I'll call you back later on." And with that, I hung up. My father was dead.

In the hours that followed, I cried. Sometimes a few tears ran down my cheeks. Other times, there were heavy sobs. Each time the crying came, though, I was still unable to identify the feeling that had triggered the response. Throughout much of the following day, an assortment of emotions each took their turn rising to the surface. There was anger— anger at the death of my father, that he dared die without offering any explanation or contrition for the actions which had wounded me so deeply. Anger that life had somehow cheated me of what I was entitled to: a loving, caring parent. Anger that he was who he was. Then came sadness.

I was sad that my father's life appeared to be a waste of humanity, a waste of flesh and blood. A waste of a being who did little more than inflict pain and suffering on those who knew him. Each of these passions rose, then subsided. I grieved the family I was born into. I cursed the life I had been given. I mourned the things that never were. These feelings I had known nearly all my life. They were all too familiar. Loneliness and abandonment soon followed.

More than a week had passed since the turtle event when my father came outside and called for me and my brothers. We weren't far away—Carter and Jack were in the field behind our house and I was climbing a tree out front near the road.

"Randy," my father shouted out the back door.

"Sir?" I answered.

"Carter—Jack," he said again.

"Sir?" they answered at the same time.

"Y'all come in here," he hollered.

"Yes sir," we all called back.

I climbed down as fast as I could and headed for the house. Carter and Jack were already inside and standing in the living room by the time I got inside.

"Y'all go on in your room," he said sternly but quietly.

I never thought about it until later that I had not seen my mother during any of this exchange. My parents hadn't been fighting or even though I had been outside I would still have heard it. This must be something good that he's going to tell us, I thought to myself.

My brothers and I sat on Carter's bed looking towards the door. None of us said a word. We just sat there staring at our daddy, wondering what was going on. It wasn't an ordinary thing for him to call us into the house—that was always Mumma's job—like for dinner and things. This must be extra special.

Daddy stood there in khaki pants and a white, short-sleeve, button-up shirt with his sleeves part-way turned up. A half-burned cigarette smoldered between his fingers. The rest of the pack was in his shirt pocket. His dark hair was combed back and, in that moment, he was at his most gentle. I remember thinking how much I loved my daddy. I loved him despite the pain and insecurity that he usually brought to my life. I loved it when he came home and walked up the sidewalk to the front door of our house. It made me feel like a regular kid. It gave me security knowing that, even though there could be trouble, my father was there. I loved it when he called me "Ran" or "Snigglefritz"—and I was loving the wonder of this moment . . . anxiously waiting to hear what my father would say.

"Ya mumma 'n I are separating," he said. His face showed no emotion or changed expression in any way. "I'm movin' out and you boys are gonna stay here 'n live with her." And with that, he left the doorway and walked back into the living room.

Carter, Jack, and I sat for a moment. Gradually, we each began crying. The three of us sat on the bed, holding and hugging each other—sobbing in uncontrollable spasms. After a few seconds, we could hear the front door open. Jack jumped up and ran into the living room.

"Please, Daddy, don't leave," he said. "I love you, Daddy, I love you—please don't leave. Can I come with you?" he continued all the while crying through his words. "Please, let me come with you! I can live with you," he said without waiting for an answer. "I can stay with you—I won't be any trouble. I promise." But Daddy walked out the front door and closed it quietly behind him.

For what seemed like hours, my brothers and I sat on our beds crying. We were certain that no matter how screwed up our world had been up to that point— whatever pleasantness there had been before had now come to an end.

If we were older children—or those of a later, less innocent generation—perhaps we would have felt less pain. But for the three of us on that Saturday afternoon in the small, white, cement-block house in Mechanicsville, it was something we could neither understand nor grasp. We only knew that our world was changing forever and that afternoon—as well as in the days and weeks that followed—no matter how many we found, there just weren't going to be enough animals to kill.

I waited another full day before finally making the drive south. The journey to Richmond always seemed to be just that, a journey. It was never just a visit home, or a trip to see family members. It was a voyage through time, a passage that led me through memories and recollections. Whenever the traffic was extra heavy, I would take the old two-lane highway three-o-one. As I crossed the Potomac, I knew the history of the area. John Wilkes Booth had fled this way after shooting Lincoln. Then, there was the drive through the rolling landscape scarred by earthworks, trenches and redoubts dug more than a century ago. And before the drive was complete, I would pass by our old farmhouse—my hands shaking while my eyes filled with tears at the thought of all that had taken place there. Throughout my drive, I considered what would be awaiting me at the funeral home. Mile after mile, I began to unfold my thoughts, having put them away so long ago like maps to a faraway place I had once visited. Eventually, I began to wonder if anyone would show up at my father's funeral. Would there be old relatives, friends, neighbors, or even those who would come to see for themselves if the old man was really dead? With only a few miles left, I decided to prepare myself for the way things would most likely be: my brothers and I alone with a few loyal relatives, standing before my father's coffin, praying for a man who died alone, unforgiving and unforgiven.

It was nearly seven o'clock in the evening when I arrived in Richmond. The funeral home parking lot was filled to near-capacity. Because it was one of the city's largest and most popular mortuaries, though, I knew other viewings would be going on at the same time as Daddy's. I parked in a far corner, tucked my shirt in, and put on a sport coat. As I walked through the front doors, an older gentleman in a black suit stood at attention. He had a droll, nondescript expression, looking like a statue with his hands crossed neatly at his waist.

"Jordan," I said. Or should I have said Jawd'n or even Jerrd'n? Just as the spelling varied every once in a while, so did the pronunciation—and I had gotten used to answering any variation of sounds. But while I could easily re-claim my Virginia accent at the drop of a hat, it could get a bit tricky with the really old folks. Having left Virginia decades ago, I sometimes had a hard time using the correct pronunciation or accent when I was speaking to an older native.

"Th' pawlor down th' hall ta th' left, suh," the greeter answered. "Mah condolences."

I looked around, doing a quick scan for a familiar face, but saw none. After only a few steps down a wide corridor, I began to hear voices. The sounds grew louder with each step. As I approached the parlor, I could see people gathered in the hall. There were so many that the entrance to the room was nearly blocked. It was filled to capacity. I wondered if I was in the right place. There were men and women of every age and even those of various colors—dark brown, light brown, very light brown, almost-white-light brown—which had always been an issue with my father.

Growing up a poor, white kid from the wrong side of the tracks seemed to give my father an added sensitivity to prejudice and bigotry. Perhaps that was the reason he never tolerated any of us in our house— my brothers or even my father's acquaintances—using slang or derogatory terms to refer to people of races different from our own. Even though we still lived, worked, played, and worshipped in what many considered the Old South, words like nigga, spook, darkie, coon or any other derogatory words with regard to those whose skin was darker than ours were simply never said or heard in our house—at least not while Daddy was sober. We only heard those words when we visited my mother's brothers. But on one particular occasion, a weekend visit to the home of one of Daddy's union buddies, my brothers and I saw just how angry the old man could get when confronted with blatant racism.

In the early 1960s, my father was working for the Western Electric Company—installing telephone switchboards for businesses and small town switching-stations for Bell Telephone in various locales throughout Virginia and Maryland. True to his roots, Daddy was a blue-collar, union man—distrustful of everyone and convinced that big business was always trying to screw every employee out of his rightful earnings. Eventually Daddy came to believe that the union—the Communication Workers of America—was out to screw him as well.

"Goddamn CWA," Daddy would say, still ranting whenever he came home from a union meeting. "They don't give a shit about the workin' man."

Once my father became disillusioned with something, it didn't take long for him to begin looking for greener pastures. It had started happening in his marriage to my mother and he was becoming disillusioned with his work life as well.

In the fall of '63, during a work stint in southern Maryland, Daddy and a couple of his co-workers attended an informal gathering at the home of a well-to-do union organizer named Bill Tyrell. But Bill Tyrell didn't work for the CWA, he worked for the Teamsters. Perhaps more importantly, though, he worked as an assistant for a man named Mr. Hoffa—and Mr. Hoffa, Bill would tell my father, wanted to help Western Electric employees get the pay and benefits they deserved.

Bill Tyrell was a nice man, at least that's the way I remember him. He was shorter than my father, probably not much taller than five and a half feet, with a paunch that he carried well. He was always well dressed, clean shaven and pleasant smelling. His hair was cut into a flat-top, cropped very close, tight against the scalp. What I remember about him best, though, was his car—a 1963 baby blue Thunderbird with a steering wheel that, with the flip of a lever, actually slid a few inches to the right to allow the driver a little extra room so as to more easily get in and out of the small car. It was a marvel to behold.

Not long after Daddy met the Teamster, Bill Tyrell's visits to our house in Mechanicsville became a regular occurrence. His visits were usually late in the afternoon and would end just after dark. And while I remember the meetings seeming quite clandestine, for the most part, Mr. Tyrell and whoever else showed up for the gatherings usually left smiling, sometimes still singing the words to a song.

"Now all for one and one for all is something you have heard," Bill, Daddy and the others in our living room would sing, "but when the Teamsters say it, the boys mean every word . . . ." As the meetings ended, the men would shake each other's hands, slap each other on the back and laugh. Bill Tyrell would always be the last to leave.

"You 'n Agnes bring the boys on up to visit us sometime," the Teamster would say as he slid into his T-bird.

"Awright," Daddy would say, "we just might do that."

My mother, my brothers and I knew we would never actually go to the Tyrell's house for a visit. It just wasn't something our family would ever do. We didn't go on vacations or travel anywhere. Daddy wasn't one who liked to visit people. But just when we thought we knew who our father was, he surprised us. One Saturday morning, my mother announced to Carter, Jack, and me that our family would be driving to Maryland to visit Bill Tyrell and his wife, Belle.

"The Tyrells have a swimmin' pool," Mumma said, hardly able to contain even her own excitement, "so pack ya bathin' suit."

"At their house?" Carter asked.

"Right in their back yard!" our mother answered.

Just after lunch, Mumma, Daddy, Carter, Jack, and I piled into the Pontiac and began the long drive from Mechanicsville to southern Maryland. Carter and Jack sat in the back seat. I sat in the front, between my mother and father. It was about a three hour drive.

When we arrived at the Tyrell's, the sun had already begun to set. My parents had planned to get to the house by late afternoon, but my father had taken one too many wrong turns. His wrong turns combined with my mother's inability to read a map—as instructed by my father—resulted in our meandering throughout the southern Maryland countryside for nearly an hour.

As soon as we arrived, both Mr. and Mrs. Tyrell took great pains to make sure we felt as welcomed as possible. Even though it was a chilly evening, my brothers and I were invited to go swimming. Jack was the only one who accepted the invitation and after a quick dip in the pool, it was time for dinner.

The inside of the Tyrell house was one of the grandest things I had ever seen. A sunken living room, marble floors, and a crystal chandelier centered high above the dining room table told us we were some place special. Instead of a collection of glasses from a box of Duz soap powder, the Tyrells had glasses with designs and plates that seemed to match. My brothers and I were on our best behavior.

After a brief prayer, we passed our plates to Mrs. Tyrell who loaded each one with several slices of roast beef, a pile of mashed potatoes and green beans. We could also have a biscuit if we wanted.

"Gravy, Jack?" she asked looking at me.

"I'm Randy," I answered.

"Oh, honey, I'm sorry," she said. "Would you like some gravy?"

"Yes, ma'am."

My parents and the Tyrells talked about the drive up and how nice the weather had been. Mrs. Tyrell spoke of how nice my brothers and I were—how lucky my mother was to have three boys. She and Mr. Tyrell had always wanted children, but had never been able. After the adults continued talking among themselves for a few more minutes, Mr. Tyrell spoke directly to Carter, Jack, and me.

"Did you boys know they'a building the longest bridge in the world?" Bill Tyrell asked.

"No, sir," we each replied.

"It's the one they'a building to send all the niggas back to Africa," he said throwing his head back in laughter. My brothers and I looked at our father, wondering how he would respond. Daddy sat silent in his chair, the corners of his mouth only turning up slightly. In the moments that followed, Bill Tyrell continued with one quip after another, all meant to degrade those whom my father would only describe as "colored." Woven throughout the man's attempts at humor were musings born deep from ignorance, hatred and bigotry, ruminations that bore no basis in reality or nature. Whenever our host paused long enough to sip his iced tea, Mrs. Tyrell would also offer her thoughts which, like her husband's, were born of prejudice. After dinner was over and the table was cleared, the Tyrells momentarily left the dining room. At that point, my father glared at my mother and declared that his children would not be sleeping under the roof of such a man. Mumma protested at first. Even if it was for one night, she said, this was the vacation she had longed for. Knowing my father, though, she quickly surrendered. When our hosts returned to the table, Daddy told the Tyrells that something had come up; we would not be spending the night. By nine o'clock, we were back in the Pontiac heading for Mechanicsville.

The ride home was filled with arguments between my parents—Mumma not understanding why my father could not accept Bill Tyrell's behavior for just one night and Daddy using every profanity he knew to debase the man he had held in such high esteem just a few hours earlier. Vulgarity spewed from my father's lip and in the midst of the madness, Daddy once again took too many wrong turns and once again we were lost in the southern Maryland countryside. Just as before, my mother unfolded a road map and turned it first one direction then another, hoping to make sense of the many colored lines that crisscrossed the paper. With their arguing near fever pitch, Mumma pleaded with my father to slow down, screaming that we would all be killed if he weren't more careful. Daddy had had enough. He reached over, grabbed the map from my mother and threw it out the window. Seated between them, I closed my eyes. I wondered if we would make it home or if we would die trying. The next morning, Mumma woke us for 12:00 Mass. We were slow rising. It had been a long night.

In the months that followed, Daddy distanced himself from Bill Tyrell and the others who had once schemed to join the Teamsters. Each Christmas, for a number of years afterward, our family would receive a card from "Bill & Belle." These many years later, I cannot say what became of them, but Daddy remained a member of the CWA. And for as long as I can remember, the old man continued to go out of his way to teach my brothers and me to be respectful and even polite to those whose skin was darker than ours.

Despite his verbal and social restraint, though, Daddy did have strong opinions about "mixin' the races," as he called it. According to my daddy's Old South way of thinking, in no way, shape or form—under no imaginable conditions or circumstances—at any time in the history of humanity were colored folks and white folks to marry or, for that matter, to even spend time together for any reason that could be considered even slightly personal. For my father, interaction between the races was to be strictly business. My father's views were widely known among the people in our neighborhood. At one point, one of the local Grand Wizards who lived just down the road from us invited Daddy to join one of Mechanicsville's local Klan groups. Daddy passed on the invitation. They later rescinded the invitation anyway when they found out we were Catholic.

"That's what happened to Cain and Abel," Daddy would say in explaining the reasoning behind his thoughts about race. "After Cain killed Abel, God struck him with the mark—made him a Negro," my father would say making sure he enunciated the word to keep us from hearing anything derogatory instead. "That's how the Negro came to be." In my father's self-educated thinking, to interact with a person of color on any level, in any matter other than business, meant to risk offending the Almighty by mingling with the descendants of Cain, the great sinner. It just wasn't meant to happen. I never did understand how my father arrived at such distorted thinking—such perverted logic. But there were a lot of things I never understood about my father.

Part Five

Elsewhere in the parlor, there were thin men and fat women, slender wives and round husbands; grown children, little girls and babies. Some people were talking, others laughing—some sobbed lightly. Each of them was engaged in some sort of discourse with another. Nearly a dozen faces, those familiar and those long forgotten, came to welcome me home, their words and presence reminding me of a time when I had a father who lived with his family. As words swirled in the air—reminiscences of a lifetime ago—I heard very little. Instead, my mind scanned the features of those in the room. Gradually, the sounds of the voices and the gestures of their bodies began to wander through my memory. The masks of age now fell from view and I recognized those I had known.

To the far left was my father's brother, Jimmy, a man who bore such an uncanny resemblance to Daddy that there was no mistaking the relation. Like my father, my uncle Jimmy had lived a blue-collar life and had survived a couple of marriages. Also like my father, Uncle Jimmy had started smoking when he was just a kid. I hadn't seen him in more than thirty years and even back then, his fingertips had begun to turn yellow, stained from the multitude of cigarettes left smoldering between his fingers every day. As strange as it seemed at the time, and I guess still does, even though he preferred smokes without a filter, my uncle would buy Winstons—which had filters. After tamping the pack on the palm of his hand for a few seconds, he would then pull out a cigarette and bite the filter off. Tucking the smoke in the corner of his mouth, he would then flip out a lighter, cup it around the end of the cigarette and start puffing away. Between every other puff or so, he would flip the end of his tongue in and out between tightly closed lips— making annoying spitting sounds as he did. The gesture was meant to spit out the tiny pieces of tobacco breaking off from the ragged end of the cigarette. Once Uncle Jimmy would leave our house after an occasional visit, my brothers and I would do our best to reproduce his tobacco-spitting action and sound—well aware that Mumma and Daddy were also annoyed by the noise.

My parents had given me the same first name as my Uncle Jimmy. My uncle had then proceeded to name his son James. His son, my cousin, named his son James and I suppose that pattern might continue until the Second Coming. When the roll is called up yonder, Jesus will need to be very specific when it comes time to sort out my relatives.

Next to Uncle Jimmy was my brother, Jack, who had arrived from Louisiana. While we were growing up, Jack had been the object of our father's disdain far too many times. From the moment of his birth until well through his adult years, Jack had been the sacrificial lamb offered by my mother to appease our father.

"I still wonder what Mumma told Daddy that day," Jack had said only a few months before as he and I were out to dinner during one of his visits with me at my home in New Jersey. While to anyone else his query would have made no sense, I unfortunately knew too well the landscape of his thoughts.

A few months after Daddy moved out in 1967, my parents sold the cement-block house where we had been living. My mother said it was because "ya father lost the house and the bank wanted their money." Whenever she was angry at Daddy, Mumma would call him "ya father," which actually seemed more as an indictment of my brothers and me for being born of such a man. In any event, I really didn't understand what she was saying. I only knew that we were moving.

The cement-block house we were leaving was nothing more than a modest bungalow, so it didn't take but a few days for my mother to pack pots and pans, glasses and plates, towels and sheets and whatever else had to be moved. There was something of my father's, though, that Mumma refused to take with us to our next home: chickens.

About a year earlier, my mother's brother, Horace, had gotten married to a middle-aged widow— Rae Nell was her name—who already had a well-established home from her previous marriage. And while our new Aunt Rae Nell was willing to love and accept my mother's brother with all his quirks and peculiarities, one thing she could not accept was the six chickens my Uncle Horace brought with him to their relationship.

"The chickens hafta go," Aunt Rae Nell had told my uncle—and within days of the pronouncement, Uncle Horace and my father had struck a deal. The chickens would roost in Mechanicsville.

"We'll sell th' eggs," Daddy told Mumma. "Make some extra money."

It may have been that Daddy was envisioning a roadside stand somewhere, perhaps set up under a tree at the end of our dead-end road or out by route three-sixty. But in the end, no one ever bought eggs from us—because we never had any to sell. For some reason, maybe it was because they didn't like the smell of dog crap from the beagles which barked at them incessantly or perhaps being away from Uncle Horace, but after just a few short weeks of arriving in

Mechanicsville, each of the six hens stopped laying eggs. Despite the fact that they were non-layers, though, we kept the hens. Carter, Jack, and I each took turns feeding them—once in the morning and then again every evening. We gave them fresh water twice a day. And early every morning, just as the sun began to peak over the trees, we would stretch a hand beneath a roosting hen and feel around for a fresh egg. There were none.

"Keep 'em," Daddy would say. "They'll start layin' again. You watch." Mumma didn't agree, but she never told him that. Finally, on a Saturday morning after Daddy had moved out, our mother called my brothers and me into the kitchen. She was sitting at the table, looking out the window toward the back yard. She seemed caught in the gaze of a distant moment. Returning to the present, she made the same pronouncement as Aunt Rae Nell had made a year before: "The chickens hafta go."

"What are we gonna do with them?" Carter asked.

"Kill 'em," our mother stated almost as a point of law. "I don't care how ya do it, but I want y'all to kill them."

Of all the Saturdays of my childhood, I can recall the events of that afternoon with more clarity than perhaps any other. I know that the sky was clear, without many clouds. The afternoon sun was hot, but not so much as to be considered uncomfortable. And once my mother had issued her decree, my brothers and I fanned out to invite the other boys living near us to come and partake in the carnage which was to bring us such perverse delight.

Within the hour, the lot of us descended upon the hens as they clucked, strutted, and flapped-about within the fence which had once been their sanctuary. Each of us chose a hen to grab. Some of the chickens ran about, scurrying from one corner of the coop to the other, flapping in hysteria. Others were instantly caught and were now being held upside-down by both feet—their wings fluttering and thrashing wildly. Before entering the pen, Carter had picked up a broken length of chain near the old dog house. He cornered one of the hens as she now clucked and flapped wildly. When she no longer had any place to run, he swung the chain. The last few metal links found their mark, curling around the poor animal's neck. The bones snapped and the first chicken was dead—far too quickly we each commented.

As the afternoon wore on, we continued our play. The second, third, and fourth chickens died in the same fashion as millions of chickens die every day. Their heads were cut off. Each of us took a turn either holding a hen or swinging the ax—with an occasional disagreement breaking out over whose turn it should be to do what. With each killing, we found the old analogy true. A chicken does run around after its head has been chopped off. The fifth chicken was killed trying to escape. It had gotten free from Brent's hands during the ax-swinging melee and was making a dash for freedom in the field behind our house. Instead of running after the hen, trying to catch it, Carter decided to get his shotgun and see if his aim was good enough to hit a quickly moving chicken. It really wasn't much of a match. The shotgun was the twelve gauge automatic Daddy had given my brother on his thirteenth birthday. Carter squeezed off three loud booms. The first two missed their mark, producing nothing but a flurry of dust and smoke. The instant the final explosion was heard, though, the spray of gunshot created a large crimson cloud which spewed into a misty dew. A burst of feathers puffed out of the cloud, then fell softly to the ground. None of what remained could be identified as a head or a leg or a wing. The chicken was gone.

The sixth bird died a slow, agonizing death. Knowing that the chicken's demise would be the end of our excitement, we relished every moment of its suffering. For the rest of the afternoon, we chased the creature through yards and fields, through creeks and marshy rushes. We struck the hen with whatever we could find. After a very long while, our chase finally took us down the short, sandy lane to Brent's house. There on the back porch sat his Grandma MacDougall.

"Whada you boys doin' ta' that chickin?" she said, her lips pursed.

"We're gonna kill it," Brent told his grandma.

"I'll take care 'a that," the old woman said as if to oblige. And with that, she pinched the bird's neck between her finger and thumb, picked it up, and wrung it. The bird was dead. Time seemed to stop at that moment and each of us stood staring at what had been the object of our enmity. During the silence, Brent's grandma had hurried into the house, now returning with a pot of boiling water and a large knife. The old woman hunkered down, pushed the dead chicken into the hot water and plucked clumps of feathers from the carcass. Once the feathers had been stripped away, she slit the chicken open and removed the innards.

"We're having chicken tonight, Brent," she said. We each looked at Brent and smiled. Whatever the rest of us were having for dinner that Saturday night, no one cared. We were just glad it wasn't chicken.

After Daddy left Mechanicsville, we moved into an old, white clapboard house that—like most large houses in Virginia—had once served as a hospital during the War Between the States. My great aunt Bertha always corrected me if I called it a "civil" war—"because there was nothing civil about it." While the house was much larger than our bungalow had been, it also had its drawbacks—namely, we had no neighbors. We wouldn't be able to listen to Buck, the man next door, beat his wife anymore on the weekends. We wouldn't be entertained listening to the four letter words we were forbidden to say. Saturday nights from our bedroom window would never be the same.

The old farmhouse sat amid thirty acres of dirt used to grow winter wheat, corn, soybeans or whatever else the landlord, Mr. Palmer, was inclined to plant. It also had one of the few small orchards left that Mechanicsville had once been known for. It was a lonely time and it made my brothers and me try to get along. For the most part, though, we each went our separate ways, each trying to escape from the reality of our family life. In future years, long after our family had moved from the farm, just the sight of the old house would make me nauseous. Even when it was our home, returning to the white clapboard house created a sense of panic and fear. The trek home after school was dreaded more than anything else—more so than long school days, difficult tests, or impossible exams. Moving to the farm had also meant changing schools. Instead of riding the school bus to St. Elizabeth's in Richmond, I now walked to the public elementary school, which was about three miles from our house.

The daily walk from the farmhouse to school led me through an assortment of settings. Once I'd reach the end of our dirt road, I would walk a short distance down Shady Grove Road—a narrow, country lane which had been traveled by Stonewall Jackson a hundred years before. After about a half-mile, I would make my way down a sandy pathway that ended at a large horse pasture. After three-quarters of a mile, I would turn south, moving quickly through the woods surrounding Gagnon's pond, all the while keeping an eye out for water moccasins and copperheads. Finally, after several more short lengths of dirt roads and muddy crossings, I would reach an open field that was part of the school grounds—the destination that would bring me respite from the turmoil of home. The afternoon walk back home would lead me through the same places I had seen in the morning, but at each spot I would stop for a moment and meander, dawdle or stroll aimlessly—anything to prolong the arrival back home.

The walk from school would ultimately return me to the foot of the hill where the long dirt road that led to our house began. There, I created a sort of ritual so as to allow myself to think I could control the chaos and violence that were such a great part of daily life. Once I had stepped from the tar-and-gravel of Shady Grove Road onto the dirt road that led to the farmhouse, I would come to a dead stop. I'd look around—sometimes asking myself if there was any place else I could go on that particular afternoon. But there never was.

Starting up the hill, I would fix my eyes downward and stare intently at my feet shuffling through the dirt and stones on the road that led to our house. If I had looked up, I would have been able to see the farmhouse gradually coming into view—first the twin chimneys, followed by the lightning rods, then the green, tin roof, and eventually the small gable at the front-center of the house. Finally, I would have been able to see the second-floor windows and the rest of the house covered with white clapboard. But if I watched my feet, instead of watching for the house as it rose above the horizon of the hill, the remainder of the day would be a time of peace and normalcy. I must not lift my eyes until I can see the house in its entirety, I would tell myself. Only then, would there be a sense of well-being for the rest of the afternoon.

In later years, therapists would assure me that such self-deception was a coping mechanism, normal behavior for children coming from families such as mine. I never knew if Carter or Jack created such imaginings for themselves. If they did, our mind games were the only thing normal about life back then.

Of the three of us, people always said that Carter would be the most successful. I suppose people could have been naturally inclined to say such a thing about him since he was the oldest. By far, he was the most compassionate and loving of us. Carter never called Mumma a bitch, as Jack once had—only to make my mother break down in tears at such a declaration from the child who almost took her life during childbirth. And whenever I was sick, like the time I was in bed with a fever from the measles, or if I ever had the flu, my oldest brother would come into the room and ask if I needed anything. One of my earliest memories is of him placing an old patchwork quilt over me as I was shaking from a fever.

"I'm so cold," I told him.

"Here, Bubba," he said spreading the quilt over my feet and tucking it neatly beneath my chin. "Anything else?"

"Uh uh."

"Try to get some sleep. You want the Teddy Bear?"

"Uh uh."

"Awright. Let me know if you need anything." And with that, my brother had established himself as the one who seemed to care about me more than any other family member ever could. It would be that way for the rest of our lives.

Jack, on the other hand, was always said to be the one most like our father. To start with, he was Jackson, junior. That tag in itself was enough to mark him forever. But there were also the physical resemblances which—later in life—were rather remarkable, including the scars on his cheeks. But when people said Jack was like my father, they weren't talking about his name or his looks. More than anything, they were talking about his temperament—particularly his willingness to fight.

On several occasions when we were growing up, both Carter and I had had temporary memory lapses when it came to dealing with our middle brother. During the course of our interchanges with one another, we would simply forget how predisposed Jack was to punching, hitting, choking, or whatever other means of inflicting pain might be available. One of the most infamous battles became the stuff of lore when a fight broke out between them while they were playing pool. Back in the late 1960s, a man had bought Mechanicsville's old feed store and replaced the bags of grain with pool tables. One day after school, Carter and Jack were playing against one another—each bragging he could out-shoot the other. As could have been predicted, my brothers began fighting and as they began swinging cue sticks at each other, Jack eventually broke one across Carter's back. After that, they weren't allowed in the pool hall anymore.

One fall Saturday afternoon, Carter made another miscalculation when he and Jack began fighting in the kitchen of the farmhouse—probably over a piece of boloney or over a last piece of cake. Mumma was not home and Daddy had not paid us a visit either. After my brothers had exchanged several coarse words, Jack threw a punch. Of course, Jack always threw the first punch. The fight then moved on to the back porch, down the stairs and into the field sloping down behind the farmhouse. I watched them for a while, but then recalled that fights could easily spread and sometimes even involve otherwise innocent bystanders—so I headed back inside for some measure of safety. After several minutes of flying fists and swinging elbows, the noise stopped. I supposed that they had finally given up on killing each other. Within a short time, Jack came through the kitchen door, his faced scraped and red, wiping blood from the corner of his mouth.

"Where's Carter?" I asked.

"Out in the garden," Jack answered. I ran to the kitchen door and could see my oldest brother lying face down among the weeds and fodder. "He's awright," Jack reassured me. "I choked him 'til he passed out. He'll wake up in a minute or two." Sure enough, within several minutes, Carter staggered back into the house. Jack had gotten our oldest brother in a choke-hold and had held on until Carter went limp. The fight was over. The following spring, I, too, would misjudge my middle brother. And while it wouldn't be the last time I would make that mistake, it was the most memorable.

Even though our parents had separated, Daddy still seemed to control the comings and goings of our daily lives, especially during the summer months. A short time after we moved into the farmhouse, our father hired some local colored men, as he called them, to sow nearly nine hundred strawberry plants on the sloping three acres or so that sat directly behind the house.

"Nine hun-erd plants?" the man in charge asked my father, enunciating every syllable. "Ya gotta tractor ta take care of 'em?" he continued.

"I got three boys," my father answered. They both laughed and then the man and his two helpers started up their old Farmall and began planting.

For a long while, Daddy had dreamed of growing a variety of fresh fruits and vegetables on our new estate. But his lack of farm knowledge prevented him from realizing that the shoots from nine hundred strawberry plants would quickly spread into the surrounding areas, producing more strawberries than any five human beings could consume in any number of seasons—no matter how voracious their appetites. And so, many of our late spring days were spent in short pants, tee shirts, and bare feet pulling weeds and picking berries.

On Saturday, we had just finished a lunch of tomatoes and mayonnaise sandwiches when my mother saw a cloud of dust rising from the dirt road leading to our house. "Ya daddy's coming," she said. "Y'all behave."

As my father's car grew closer, the cloud of dust grew larger and began to billow, signaling the approach of a coming storm. Carter, Jack, and I left the kitchen and went out the back door to meet Daddy when he arrived. Mumma followed behind us at a distance, stopping at the top of the stairs that led down to grass.

Slowly, his big, green Pontiac made its way through the sand and dirt path that led to the back of the house.

"Hey Daddy," we all said greeting our father as he slowly got out of the car. There was a pause in the greeting as he stared toward the field to see how many red berries lay shining in the sun.

"Hey boys," he responded, "whadya doin'?"

"Not much," Carter answered.

"Goddamn, I can see that," Daddy said as he swung the car door closed. Quickly, our father hobbled over towards the ridge overlooking the slope where the strawberries grew. His childhood bout with polio had not only shortened his leg, but had begun to gnarl his foot as well—causing his limp to give way to a hobble. Despite his inability to run, though, my brothers and I knew that our father was still a force to be reckoned with.

"You boys get your asses over there right now and start pickin' strawberries," he said.

"Jackson," our mother interrupted, "they picked strawberries all morning. Can't those wait another day?"

"Hell no," Daddy answered. "I want them picked

right now." And with that, my brothers and I walked into the field as our parents made their way into the house.

Knowing there really weren't a lot of berries to be picked, Carter, Jack, and I took our time. Besides, we would much rather have been outside in the field than in the house listening to our father's ranting. As we squatted down over one plant after another, I eventually began to think that maybe we could be having more fun doing this than we had realized. I waited for a moment, then gradually moved away from my brothers towards one of the rows located at the edge of the field. I knew that if I was going to play war with my brothers—especially Jack—I would need an ample supply of dirt clods, and the edge of a field was always where the most clods were.

Slowly, trying not to give notice, I knelt down on one knee and pretended as if I was picking a berry. After another moment, I picked up a fist-sized dirt clod and threw it at Jack while his back was to me. I knew my aim was good and my throw was hard as the clod hit him squarely in the back, breaking into pieces as it struck him. It was also at that very minute that I realized what a mistake I had made. In my deep, intense desire and scheming to have fun, I had forgotten Jack's deep, intense desire to inflict pain. So as the hard, sunbaked clay broke into pieces in the middle of my brother's back, a broad smile came across his face. It was his turn to get me.

In a panic, I began throwing whatever I could find, hoping that something would make him think twice before coming at me in force, but there was no stopping him. He searched the ground around him and found the hardest clods. One, two, three, four—the fists of dirt kept coming—stinging as they struck my back and side. I ducked down as low as I could until my face was nearly touching the ground. After a minute or two, I began to think that maybe the worst had passed. *Surely he knows how bad my side is hurting now. Surely he believes we're even now.* I raised my head.

I was never really sure how it worked, but for some reason it always takes a few seconds between the time something hits a body—such as a rock-hard dirt clod—and when it finally begins to register with the brain that something is wrong, that pain has arrived. It's a mystical moment, a fleeting period when one begins to think that maybe there won't be any pain at all.

As I raised my head to see what Jack's intentions were, I saw a glimpse of rock-hard, red clay quickly coming at my head much too fast for me to move out of its way. It hit me like the boulder it was and, sure enough, it was immediately followed by that mystical moment when I tried to deny that any pain might follow. As I lay on the ground, I looked at the blue, cloudless sky and waited for the pain to arrive. Instead, the first sensation I noticed was a metallic taste in my mouth. I thought it might be the taste of Virginia dirt. But as I wiped my mouth, I noticed that the back of my hand was covered with blood—and with that, the mystical moment came to an end.

My head was throbbing. I climbed to my feet while Jack was still throwing dirt clods at me. Tears streamed down my cheeks. I made a run for the only place I thought I might be safe, somewhere I knew he would not come after me—inside the house. In my eleven year old mind, I could only focus on the immediacy of the pain and the blood. The horror of our battle had caused me to forget that, while I might be safe inside the house, my father was there also. So with saliva and blood oozing through the fingers of my hand as I covered my mouth, I ran up the wooden stairs that led on to the back porch.

Once I reached the top of the stairs, I darted around an assortment of obstacles. Yet, while I had successfully cleared the largest obstacle—a small barrel of dry milk—I still managed to trip on the corner of a twenty-five pound bag of dog food, falling heavily against the dirty, white kitchen door. With tears now flowing freely down my face, I removed my hand and grasped the porcelain door knob that would let me into the kitchen. The more I wrestled with the door knob, the more slippery it became from the saliva and blood that covered my hand. Finally, the door began to open, as if by itself. But in a second, I realized that my mother had opened it from inside the kitchen.

"What happened to you?" she asked as she drew back with some measure of disgust at seeing the mess of my face. My father sat at the small kitchen table sipping a cup of coffee. He only looked at me in silence.

"Jack hit me with a dirt clod," I blurted through the blood and tears. I really hadn't intended to accuse my brother. God knows that I had seen him suffer at my father's hands too many times. If anything, I was the one who had started the whole thing. In answering my mother's question, I had only meant to explain what had happened. And yet for most of my life, now, I have secretly wondered what it was—what word did I say, what notion did I imply, what curse did I unleash that day that caused my father to react the way he did.

"See," Mumma said glaring at my father. As soon as the word came out of her mouth, my father jumped up from his chair and began his tirade.

"Goddamn that boy," he said to whoever was listening. "I'm gonna beat his ass." My father got up and hobbled through the kitchen door, across the porch, and was headed down the back stairs. I stood there not knowing what to expect. For their part, once they had seen I was bleeding, Carter and Jack had started to make their way back to the house from the strawberry fields. As it turned out, my brothers' concern brought them to the back stairs just as Daddy was coming down. Perhaps if Jack had not been so concerned—if he had not come up to the house—he would have still been out in the field when Daddy came after him. That way, he could have easily out-run our father. But it just didn't happen that way.

As they started up the stairs, Daddy lunged forward and grabbed Jack's wrist, gripping him tightly. Then in a single, seemingly-effortless motion—as if he had practiced it a thousand times—while holding my brother's arm with one hand, Daddy unfastened his own belt with his other hand, and yanked it from the loops of his pants. Knowing what was coming, Jack began pleading with my father, desperately trying to hold back the rage that was mounting against him.

"Daddy, I didn't mean to . . . please don't."

Ignoring my brother's cries, Daddy began whipping Jack—slowly at first, as if he was trying to find his mark, then striking him with greater accuracy and deliberation with each successive swing of the belt.

"Daddy. Please."

"Goddamn you, boy."

"Please, Daddy—Daddy, please. Stop."

The thin narrow belt made loud cracking noises each time it snapped against the exposed skin of my brother's bare legs. As the whipping grew more intense, Daddy began sweating while spit sprayed from his mouth. He continued to curse and swear at my brother. Blood had now begun weeping through the cuts and welts that appeared on Jack's legs.

"You son of a bitch."

"Daddy, I'm sorry . . . ."

And my father continued.

"You gonna . . . ," my father said. Daddy now swung the belt so hard that he seemed unable to remember what it was he was going to say. His arm flung the strap wildly, yet each time still managing to hit his mark.

"You gonna do it again?" he asked after a few more strikes. Jack was now in such pain and crying so uncontrollably that he could barely answer.

"Jackson, that's enough," my mother said without much effect.

A moment or two later, our father stopped, exhausted from the ordeal. Jack collapsed to the ground—unable to fully understand what had just happened or why.

Jack stood in the corner of the funeral parlor. People sometimes said my brother went to Louisiana to get away from our father's fields, to provide him with the escape he longed for. But I knew better. There was no way to escape Daddy. At least I never found one.

Part Six

Not far from Jack, I could see the unmistakable bald head of my brother, Carter. As the oldest son, Carter was the one in charge of the funeral arrangements. For years, as Daddy had come close to dying once, twice, or ten more times—Carter became our father's mentor in settling his personal affairs. In the years when my father had accumulated stocks and bonds, treasury bills and retirement accounts, Carter was the one the old man confided in—wanting to make sure the remainder of all his earthly belongings would be distributed according to his wishes. This child would get a lot "because he came to see me when I was sick," Daddy would decree. Another child would get nothing because he or she had turned away from the abusive old man. Ironically, there would be no inheritance to be had—only empty bank accounts and a mountain of medical bills accumulated from years of poor health. There wasn't even enough money for a grave marker. In the end, it seemed that the only thing my brother could do would be to make excuses for his father's failings. And that was something he had done many times before.

Farmhouses built in the early nineteenth century had only one source of heat—a fireplace. Our old farmhouse had two of them, each with a massive chimney strategically located on either side of the main floor. Families would constantly stock up on enough chopped wood so as to at least have a small fire constantly burning—if not for heating the house, then certainly for cooking. During the colder months, the fires would burn much brighter so as to heat not only the main floor, but the upstairs as well. Getting heat from the first floor to the upstairs—when there were no fireplaces on the second floor—required some ingenuity. To facilitate this, small openings of about one square foot would be cut in the ceiling of the first level all the way through the floor on the second level. The openings would then be covered with a metal grate—often made of tin—which would be decorative while allowing the heat from the fireplaces to rise through to the upstairs bedrooms. A rather simple design that was very effective.

By the time we moved to the farm in 1967, the fireplaces had been replaced by oil burning stoves. Too bad, really, as we often ran out of heating oil because my mother didn't have enough money to keep the burners going. Had the fireplaces still been open and able to burn wood, we would have had fewer cold days and freezing nights in a clapboard structure which was already quite drafty. Yet, while the fireplaces had been replaced, the venting holes in the upstairs floors were still there. On more than one occasion, they made for serious entertainment as Carter, Jack, or I would pull off the metal grates and stick our heads through the holes. Eventually, we were able to do this quietly enough so as to have our heads sticking out of the downstairs ceiling. Again, more than once, we were able to scare the daylights out of our mother or whoever else was downstairs sitting in the living room. There was no need for screams or making scary noises; a simple, slow, deep-voiced "hello" coming from a head sticking through the ceiling was enough to set my mother to cursing and swearing that she was on the verge of a heart attack.

I was eleven years old when, as usual, a familiar cloud of dust made its way down the dirt road that led to our house. Looking out the window of the bedroom Jack and I shared, I could see the familiar green of Daddy's car making its way down the lane. The day had already started off poorly, particularly for my mother. Quite early in the morning, she had received a phone call from her brother, Donald. He had news about his sister-in-law, Tammy.

Tammy Hickman was my uncle's sister-in-law. She was a short woman, smaller than average, but not necessarily petite, nor was she overweight either. Even though I was just a kid, I could see what made her attractive. Her light brown hair was chopped short, a straight-across cut that ended just above her neck. Tomboyish, maybe, but her face was more feminine than not and without blemish or flaws of any kind. Dotted with a few freckles from where the sun had kissed her small nose, she was definitely pretty. What made her most attractive, though, was the smile which revealed a perfect set of white teeth. Tammy, as we were allowed to call her, had a pleasant, infectious laugh that was so pleasing to the ear that my brothers and I would try to say something funny just to hear her laugh. Tammy had come to Virginia from Louisiana, so her speech was a bit different from ours, as she would say her husband Paul was "woikin" instead of "wurkin" or, if nature called, she would ask to use the "ba'trum" instead of the bathroom. It was a delight when she visited.

Cherries are one of the first fruits of the growing season and Tammy knew this. One Saturday before school had let out for the summer, she stopped by the farmhouse and asked if she could pick some cherries from our trees. She was planning to make pies.

"Of course," my mother told her, otherwise—as it did nearly every season—the fruit would just have fallen to the ground and rotted. Growing strawberries was quite enough to keep me, my brothers, and our mother busy. We had absolutely no interest in dealing with the cherries.

"Take as many as you want," Mumma said. "We won't be eating them this year." My mother laughed.

"I'll tell you what," Tammy answered back. "I'll take enough to bake you a pie, too."

"It's a deal," Mumma replied.

True to her word, Tammy returned to our house the very next day with a large, warm cherry pie wrapped in a tea towel. With her two small children in tow, they didn't stay long.

"Joe's waitin' at home," Tammy said. "We need ta get back. Thanks so much, Agnes. I really appreciate it." After packing her two little ones back into the car, Tammy smiled the perfect smile and said our names aloud.

"Jack . . . ," she said pointing at me.

"No ma'am, I'm Randy."

She laughed. "I never kin git you boys' names straight." Her delightful laugh continued. "We'll see you all later. Thanks so much, Agnes." And with that she left. We never saw her again.

"Somethin' happened last night," Donald said as my mother picked up the phone, before she had the chance to say anything.

"What's wrong?" Mumma asked.

"Tammy's dead," my uncle answered.

"What? Oh my Gawd!"

"Paul shot 'n killed her. He was drunk. They had 'n argument. Kids were right there in the livin' room. He shot her in the head while they were watchin'."

"Oh my Gawd!" my mother said.

"I'll let ya know about th' funeral plans as soon as I know somethin'." With that, he hung up. Later that afternoon, my father came visiting.

Since it was widely understood that the old man could have already had more than a few beers on his drive to our house, instead of going down to meet my father, I decided to wait and listen through the hole in the floor of my room to see if I should come downstairs or seek some means of escape. If he was half-drunk when he arrived, it wouldn't take long before he was full-drunk. For my brothers and me, half-drunk arrivals meant ducking out of a window or sneaking out the door before Daddy caught sight of us. Once out of the house, we could hunker-down in the woods for a few hours and wait until our father left again.

As I sat on the floor of my room, I could hear the back door open and my father's familiar hobble as he made his way to the kitchen table. With his voice loud and filled with goddamns and shits, my mind took to survival mode. I grabbed a long sleeve shirt thinking that I might need it if I had to stay in the woods late into the evening. Jack was already outside, so I knew he was already out of harm's way. Carter, on the other hand, had been sitting in the living room watching television. Mumma was in the kitchen with Daddy.

As I sat next to the hole in the floor of my room, I listened intently—trying to decide the best time to make my escape. I could hear my parents talking. Their voices were muffled and subdued. Gradually, though, their speech grew in intensity and had now become loud enough for me to hear every nuance of their exchange.

"Hey boy, come here," Daddy shouted at Carter. "Ya wanna know why I don't live here anymore?"

My brother got up from his chair, stepped through the doorway of the living room and into the kitchen where my parents were.

"Sir?" Carter asked not sure what his response should be.

"Ya wanna know why we got divorced?" my father shouted. Nearly every word slurred from his mouth.

"Jackson," my mother yelled.

"Le'me tell ya wha' happened . . . ," Daddy kept on.

"Jackson. Stop!"

"A-a-after ya brother Rusty died," my father stammered and slurred, "ya mumma wouldn't let me get between her legs any more. Sh-sh-she became a cold bitch . . . ."

"Daddy, stop," Carter now pleaded.

"Jackson, stop it," my mother shouted again.

After my father gave graphic detail of his and Mumma's bedroom life, he concluded the tirade. "Truth hurts, dudn' it?" Daddy said with a perverted sense of pride. "It's ya mumma's fault . . . all this shit. She didn' wanna be a wife to me anymore. She wouldn' have sex with me . . . made me go somewhere else to get it."

"Oh, Daddy," Carter said through his tears.

"Goddamn this shit. Goddamn you."

I could hear my mother sobbing heavily. I wasn't sure if she was crying from the pain of the moment, or from the news of Tammy's murder, or perhaps both. Perhaps some small part of her wished her life would end just as quickly as Tammy's had.

A moment later, I could hear the back door open, followed by clumsy footsteps. The car started up. Our father was gone.

Whenever similar occasions followed, Carter would be quick to defend the old man. "He didn' mean it," he would say in an attempt to explain Daddy's cruel words. "He was jus' drunk." As usual, Carter was partly right. Daddy was drunk.

Glancing around the parlor, I wondered how long it had been since Carter, Jack, and I had gathered together amidst so many old familiar faces. Even at the last family wedding, one of us had been missing. Now, as I moved across the room, I could hear Jack's distinct laughter filling the room like a sweet fragrance.

As children, there had been too few times when my brothers and I had laughed together. This evening, though, as Carter found humor in something whispered not far from where the remains of our father lay, I thought of the farmhouse where we suffered through our teen years—and on one occasion, the laughter we experienced at our father's expense.

Only a few weeks had passed since Daddy had given Jack the whippin' we would always remember. Again, my brothers and I were in the small yard in back of the farmhouse doing whatever we could to while away the hours of a summer afternoon. Earlier in the week, Daddy had stopped at the house and dropped off about half a dozen large sacks filled with rolls of thick telephone cable. With each bag weighing nearly a hundred pounds or so, the sacks still sat where Daddy had unloaded them—in a patch of dirt behind a small, white shed that had once been a smokehouse.

With the sounds of cicadas echoing, we once again noticed a large cloud of dust rising from the dirt road to our house. This time, though, the cloud seemed to be much larger than usual, puffing furiously and rising higher than was customary. After several moments, we could make out the unmistakable shape of the green Pontiac. Daddy was coming—and he was coming fast.

In just a minute, our father had driven his car to the back of the house. The vehicle had hardly managed to finish its bouncing and swaying from the potholes in the dirt path when he pushed open the car door and began hobbling across the grass. He was heading for the stack of bags behind the smokehouse.

"Bury the shit!" he said pointing and shouting.

My brothers and I looked at each other, not sure what was happening or what our father was talking about. By this time, Mumma had come out of the house to see what was going on.

"What's wrong?" she asked. She shouted toward my father who was now nearly behind the smokehouse.

"We gotta bury this shit," he screamed. Saliva was foaming from the corners of his mouth.

"Whadya talkin' about?" Mumma asked.

"They'a after me," Daddy hollered with a look of both fear and panic on his face. "We need to get rid of these bags. We gotta bury 'em."

During his trip from wherever he had come that afternoon, our father must have thought about where the bags would be buried because he wasted no time pointing out the exact location of where we should start digging. Our parents dragged each of the sacks towards the entrance to the crawl space beneath the farmhouse. A thick, white, plywood door—about three foot high and three foot wide—led to an empty span of dirt that spread out beneath our house. Carter opened the white, plywood access door and then the three of us crouched low and duck-walked into low space. Once there, we began using shovels and other garden tools to dig a hole large enough to accommodate the bags of cable.

Despite our father's demands that we dig as fast as we could, Carter, Jack, and I looked at each other with slight smiles. Never before had we seen our father scared. Never before had we seen him appear so alone and vulnerable. Never before had we enjoyed anything related to our father so much as we enjoyed that moment.

With each bag of cable that Daddy passed to us, he seemed to shake more and more. Sweat poured down his face and chest. "They'a gonna lock my ass up," he would say over and over again as he hobbled back and forth fetching bags of cable from behind the smokehouse. After we had buried the last load, Daddy stood in the yard, staring down the dirt road, waiting for a cloud of dust to indicate that someone was coming after him. Carter and Jack used a rake and their hands to smooth over the dirt covering the cable so that the ground would appear undisturbed. Once we had crawled out, Daddy closed the door—securing it with a new padlock—and just as quickly as he had driven down the long dirt road, he sped off, his tires spitting out sand and small rocks. At the same time, Mumma made her way up the stairs and returned to the kitchen. My brothers and I stood watching our father's car disappear in a cloud of dust. Within a moment, we began to laugh, slightly at first, then hard and heavy.

Whatever had spawned Daddy's fears of jail time, we never did find out. Maybe the years of theft from the telephone company—not only bags of copper cable, but an assortment of tools, telephones, and other equipment as well—had worn on him to the point where paranoia had begun to set in. Whatever the reason, it was a day we would always remember. Not because anyone ever came to lock Daddy up—but because for just a few minutes, the old man carried the same burden of fear that Carter, Jack, and I had borne far too long. It was a good day.

At very young ages, my brothers and I learned that we did not always have to be victims. I had watched—and even been a willing participant—as my friends, brothers and I had tortured all kinds of creatures. But for me, there was a line which had not been crossed. Aside from shooting an occasional squirrel or rabbit while hunting, I had never intentionally killed an animal—alone, on my own. I had never stood in silence and watched a creature die. I never imagined that I could or would. It was not who I was.

Living on a farm always meant having lots of dogs around. None of them were purebreds by any stretch. There were no pedigrees, only mangy mutts that barked and yelped whenever a rabbit or deer or cat or skunk happened by. My mother wanted at least a couple of them around—it made her feel safe I suppose. Whenever one of the females became "in heat," as Mumma would call it, we would confine the animal in a small space beneath the house (in the same crawl space where we had buried the cable)—making sure the animal got plenty of food and water—for the length of time she was in season. After the bitch had stopped bleeding, we would let her out. At least, that was the plan, but it didn't always work that way.

In July of 1968, one of our smaller dogs, a beagle, appeared to be a bit swollen around her midsection. Neither my brothers nor I had noticed, but on one of his visits to the farm, Daddy had seen her and told my mumma that something had to be done.

"You're gonna have a shit load of dogs running around here if you don't," he said as he got into his big green Pontiac. "Next time I come back, I don't wanna see a bunch of goddamn dogs here. Nobody's gonna buy 'em—they'll all be mutts."

"I know, Jackson," Mumma said as a matter of fact.

"Tell Carter to drown the puppies soon as they come out. Put 'em all in a crocus sack with a cinder block. Throw 'em out in the pond."

"I know."

"Don't need a bunch 'a goddamn mutts." And with that, Daddy closed the car door and headed down the long dirt road away from our house.

"You heard ya daddy," Mumma said to Carter as he, Jack, and I stood there watching our father's car disappear in a cloud of dust.

"Awright," Carter said. As he had gotten older and whenever our father wasn't around, my brother had begun to dispense with the "yes, ma'ams" and "no ma'ams" which had been obligatory for most of our lives.

A few weeks later, as the summer sun began to set, the beagle lay curled in the corner of one of the outbuildings—just a few feet from an old combine Mr. Palmer used to harvest soybeans. Carter stood next to the dog—crocus sack in hand—waiting for the last of the litter to make its way through the birth canal.

"I think she's done," he said. "It's gittin' dark and if I wait too long, she's not gonna let me take 'em away from her." He scooped up the tiny whimpering pups by the scruff of the neck and placed them in a sack one at a time. Their eyes were still closed, their faces and snouts still wrinkled. My brother didn't say much. He just did what our father had told him to do.

Figuring that the momma beagle had finished delivering, I scooped her up in my arms and carried her to the back porch of our old farmhouse. She was exhausted. As I cradled her, she lifted her head, not sure what I was doing. But if animals are capable of trust, I suppose she trusted me. She relaxed as much as she could.

By the time I reached the steps up to the porch, my right leg had begun to feel warm. With her in my arms, there wasn't much I could do to see what was causing it, but after laying the momma down in the porch corner, I noticed that my shorts and leg were covered in blood. She was still giving birth.

I placed her on an old pile of rags and, as I did, a pup slid from her womb, followed by another. I stood there looking—lost in the moment.

"Why'd you bring her up here?" Carter asked as he climbed the steps to the porch.

"I thought she might like it up here, be more comfortable."

"Shit," he said after staring at her for a brief moment. "Where'd those other pups come from?"

"She hadn't finished when you left," I said. "She had two more."

"I guess I'll have to take them in the morning."

"No, you're not," I said.

"Randy, Daddy said they had to go."

"You're not drowning them. No more crocus sacks. No more puppies in the pond."

Mumma had heard us yelling at each other. Coming out the kitchen door, she turned on the dim light bulb that hung from the middle of the porch ceiling.

"What's wrong?" she said. "Look at you. You've got blood all over you."

"It's okay, Mumma," I answered as a matter of fact. "It's not mine. I brought her up here, but I didn't know she wasn't finished. Mumma, there's two puppies left. We can't drown them, too."

"But Daddy said . . . ." Carter shot back.

"We can keep those two," Mumma answered. "At this point, two more won't make much of a difference."

"We can leave them up here on the porch," she continued. "You go get in the tub. You smell awful."

The back porch of the farmhouse had always been a catch-all for everything imaginable. From old coats, to old boots, brooms, rakes, wooden boxes, an assortment of hand tools, such as saws and hammers, and even a few 50 pound bags of powdered milk Daddy had brought home and Mumma served at nearly every meal. There were also large sacks of flour and sugar, and even a few fishing poles scattered about. Now—tucked in the corner amidst a pile of smelly rags and dog shit—were a momma beagle and her two pups.

After a few weeks, the pups had learned the layout of the large porch and had even begun playing hide-n-seek with one another. Whenever someone opened the kitchen door, one of them would occasionally let out a high-pitched yelp as it got caught underfoot with its paw getting stepped on or its tail nearly getting caught in the door.

"You need to fix it where they can't get under my feet or in the house," Mumma told me. "You wanted to keep 'em. Now take care of 'em and make it so they can't get in here."

Later that day, I stacked a few sacks of dried milk, flour, and sugar on top of one another—creating a barricade between one end of the porch and the area leading to the kitchen door. I hoped that the pups would not be able to climb over it. It worked.

"Good job, James Randolph," my mother said late the next morning as she left to go to the store. "Maybe next week, we can put them down in the yard. Right now, they are still so little they could get under the car and you wouldn't even see 'em, 'specially that one with the brown spot on his back."

Carter and Jack were gone that day. Where, I don't remember. It really doesn't matter anyway.

Mumma was gone. Daddy had not been around in more than a week. There were no friends with me. No neighborhood kids. I was completely alone.

I stood on the porch watching the pups play. The larger one—with black and brown patches across his face—was chewing on an old piece of rope. The smaller one was next to me, just on the other side of the barricade I had made. I had wanted to pick the little fellow up. I had wanted to hold him, to pet him and scratch behind his ears. I thought of how handsome a dog he would make. As I reached over the barricade, one of the large sacks slid from the top and fell directly on the pup, landing squarely in the middle of its back.

"Oh, shit," I screamed. "Oh my God. Oh damn. Oh shit." I threw my leg over the barricade and quickly lifted the bag off the puppy. He lay there unable to move. His eyes were open. His cries were loud. His back was broken. I scooped him up in my hands and he continued to cry even more loudly. Within a moment or two, his yelps turned into wailing. His whimpers became deep moans of pain. *Maybe it would have been better if the sack of flour had fallen on his head*, I told myself. *Then he wouldn't have felt anything.* But it hadn't, and he was still alive.

All these years later, I still wonder if what I did next was the right thing. I still wonder if I had the right to do it. If I should have done it. If there were other options that I could have considered. But I was twelve years old. And sometimes twelve year old boys don't always know the right thing to do.

I carried the pup as carefully as I could, trying not to cause him anymore pain, but nothing seemed to help. I looked for a spot behind one of the outbuildings where the ground would be soft—soft enough to dig and dig quickly. I laid the pup on the ground and ran to get a shovel. I dug quickly. I dug deep. About two feet down and a foot across. Then, as tears poured down my face, I picked up the wailing creature and laid him at the bottom of the pit. Wanting to make sure he would not lie in the pit and continue crying, I fetched a cinder block and held it high directly over the whimpering pup. I centered the block as best I could, wanting to hit my target most effectively. I dropped the concrete block. After a deep thud, he was quiet. I filled the hole with dirt. I had done it. Without friends. Without my brothers. Without anyone looking on or whispering in my ear. I had decided when death should come. I had done what I had never thought I could. The sin was mine alone. I still think of that day and sometimes, either rightly or wrongly, I wonder if God allows things to happen as punishment for all of the misdeeds we commit—even the things we simply allow to happen—things which are so sinful, we forever hold them as secrets. I'm still not sure.

Part Seven

My brothers and I were all Boy Scouts. Every other Thursday night our troop met in the fellowship hall at the Methodist Church in Mechanicsville. Carter, Jack, and I were allowed to go as long as we did not step foot inside the church. It was, after all, a Protestant building. It also helped that there was no Catholic church in Mechanicsville, so there wasn't even a remote opportunity to join a troop that met at a Catholic church. It simply didn't exist. So as far as sin was concerned, we were covered.

The scoutmaster, George Whitecloud, was a kind, caring, father-figure who was part Cherokee—which made our time with him all the more entertaining. On Thursday nights, after the business of scouting and merit badges had been dispensed with, Mr. Whitecloud would embark on an animated re-telling of myth and legend, recounting tales of the Indians who had settled Virginia a thousand years before.

With a Chesterfield dangling from the side of his mouth, he would tell of great chiefs and braves buried in sacred mounds of earth hidden away in the nearby Chickahominy Swamp. He would utter their sacred names and would assure us that the ghosts of those long dead still roamed the wetlands. I cannot describe the thrill and pleasure such a caring man brought into our lives amidst what would have been an otherwise dreary existence.

For kids in rural Virginia, being a Boy Scout was the best way to get to know other kids and—perhaps most importantly—to get to know the kind of men who treated kids halfway decently, men who didn't smack us or take a belt after one of us. It was also a way to get to know boys from other parts of the region, far from our neighborhoods and even far from Richmond. It was an opportunity to make new friends, to meet boys from the mountains to the west of us and the Tidewater region to the east. And in the summer of 1969, we also met boys who were, in too many ways, like ourselves.

I never was a good swimmer. Whenever a group of us went to a lake or a pond for relief from the summer sun, I stayed close to the shore or, if there was a chance the water was too deep, I wouldn't go in at all. *Perhaps if I had been a swimmer, I could have out-swum them*, I would tell myself for years afterward. *If only I had known how to swim, I could have saved myself from so much embarrassment and shame*. But it didn't happen that way.

"Jordan," Harold D shouted, "get on down to the lake. Everybody else is gone." Harold D. Ashburn— "Harold D" as we called him—was the assistant scoutmaster. It was his job to stay with the campsite whenever all of the scouts, as well as the scoutmaster and other adults, had left for an activity. It was also his job to make sure every boy participated, whether we liked the water or not.

"Awright," I answered. "I'm headin'."

It had taken nearly two hours for the troop to make the drive to Bear Creek Lake near Cumberland, Virginia, where the Jamboree was being held that year. We had arrived late in the morning, set up our tents and eaten lunch. After cleaning mess kits, washing pots and pans, and getting personal gear squared away, hundreds of scouts had begun the short walk to the lake, eager to dive off piers and cool off in the green water.

I made the walk slowly, purposely lagging behind in hope of foregoing the water activity completely.

"It'll probably be too deep for me to swim to 'em anyway," I had told one of my friends. But in the end, Harold D had told me I needed to go.

By the time I reached the lake, my troop had already gotten into the water. The lake seemed to spread out from one end of the horizon to the other, filled with at least two hundred splashing bodies and bobbing heads. My friends, though, were nowhere to be seen. I decided to walk through the shallow shoreline—all the while looking for familiar faces. But there were none. Finally, after scanning the lake for few minutes, I could see one of my friends standing on a floating pier about fifty yards into the lake.

"It looked like the water was so shallow you could almost walk to the pier," I explained years later. So that's what I decided to do.

"I was almost there," I recalled, "when some boys called out to me—sayin' stuff like 'hey come here, we wanna talk to you.' I was tryin' to ignore them, but they just kept coming closer."

"I was about thirty feet from the pier when they caught up to me. That was also when the water got real deep. I started doing my best to swim to the pier, but these boys could swim better than me. There were three of 'em." Even though many years have passed since the experience, the child inside of me still has trouble explaining what happened. He has trouble understanding why it still affects so much of his life, how he thinks, who he trusts, what risks he will or will not take. It is still too much a part of him.

I began swimming, aiming for the pier, hoping to reach it before the unknown boys would reach me. Even though I was paddling and kicking as best I could, the reality was that I was barely treading water. Within a moment, they had caught up to me. Now there was one boy to my right and another to my left. A third was directly behind me. The boys at my side grabbed my arms and held them firmly—allowing me to neither swim nor punch. All the while, I kept kicking and struggling just to stay afloat. While those at either side were laughing, the kid directly behind me wrapped his arms around my chest—squeezing and pulling at my nipples. After a second, the body in back of me pulled me tightly to him, pressing himself into the center of my buttocks. He then slid his hands from my chest down to my waist, working feverishly to strip off my swimming trunks. Deep guttural moans rose from his mouth as he began to breathe heavily. My heart was racing. Within a moment, I moved passed panic to abhorrence and disgust. I was now fighting for what was left of my sanctity. What my father had not taken from me, I wasn't going to give to some horny boy scout. With lake water pouring down my throat, I kicked hard in every direction. Perhaps because of my anger or because of my own desire for survival—or because the boys at my side had become caught up in their own sexual excitement—I was able to push myself high enough out of the water to scream.

"Help!"

As soon as the word left my mouth, a man on the nearby pier jumped in and swam toward me. With that, the three strangers pushed me away and were never seen again.

I never spoke about the incident. I never told my scoutmaster or Harold D. I never told my friends, or my parents, or my brothers. We each had our own trials and we each carry our own secrets. Whether they involve young boys or our own fathers, sometimes the easiest thing to do is not talk about them at all.

On the other side of the funeral parlor stood a tall fellow about my age. His lack of hair would have hidden him from my memory, but as a broad smile and crooked teeth showed across his face I knew in a moment it was my childhood friend, Earl.

Earl had lived across the road from us when I was about eight years old. He was Vaughn and Mabel Stewart's oldest son. Besides Earl, they had another boy, Charles, who was my age. Besides being afflicted with cerebral palsy, Charles was also mentally retarded. Charles always wanted to play with Earl and me—but he wasn't able. He would try running and even try skipping, laughing with delight as he tried to lift his feet from the ground—but he would fall or his metal leg braces would get tangled and clang together. Earl would stop and pick his brother up. Charles would be crying, but in the tenderest of moments Earl would wipe his tears and Charles would say in the most innocent and gentlest manner, "Thank you, brother." It was an old-fashioned way of addressing a sibling, but Charles did it out of love rather than pretense.

Unlike Earl, Charles always wore short pants whenever the weather was even close to being warm. I suppose it was easier for him to get pants on if they were shorts. The legs that stuck out beneath his shorts were thick and twisted. Large scars ran down the shins of both limbs. The scars seemed to be about an inch wide, although I never really measured them. They were lines running down each leg with dots on both sides of the lines, as if someone had taken a large pen and drawn deep brown vertical marks and put tiny circles about two inches apart on each side of those lines. For me, it was the strangest thing I had ever seen. It reminded me of the kind of scars the creature had in the Frankenstein movies. But I never said anything. I would just catch a glance every chance I could—but not long enough to be grossed out by them. "Look, but don't stare," Mumma would always say.

Sometimes I think Earl resented Charles. Not because he occasionally had to take care of his younger brother, but because it was Earl who always got any of the whippings Vaughn liked to dish out. It was sort of an unspoken rule among all the kids that I knew that parents—daddies when they were around and mummas when they had to—had a certain amount of whippings to hand out every other day or so. Carter got his regular share. Jack got his regular share. I got mine and Earl got his and so on. But then there were the extenuating circumstances when some boys would get more than their share. That's what happened with Earl. Vaughn would want to hit Charles something, but then Mabel would be standing there and just say his name, "Vaughn"—as if she was yelling at a dog that was barking too loudly. And Vaughn would lower his hand or put away his belt if he was getting ready to swing it.

Later on, after Mabel had held back his hand, after she had restrained all the passion Vaughn had felt—all the power he had drummed up so as to hit Charles—he would take it out on Earl. I guess that was why a boy who could be so devoted to his brother could be so cruel to other creatures. And one morning that summer, I began to understand my friend.

Like my father, Vaughn was a drinker. And like my father, he liked to throw his might into the whippings he gave his children from time to time. Even though it was supposed to be "the whippin' of ya life"—as Vaughn always called it right before he started—Earl got them on a regular basis.

One morning, after Earl had had a whipping, he showed up at my front door. It was early and I was just coming outside. Earl was standing there wearing shorts which, despite the hot weather, was unusual for him. His legs had pink welts from his shins up to just above his knees. I didn't have to ask what they were. I had seen them enough before.

"Whadya wanna do?" I asked as we walked away from the house.

"Let's go find somethin'," he said.

"Like what?" I asked again.

"There are some blue jay nests in the pine woods," he explained. "I wanna see if we can get them."

It was August and school would be starting in a few weeks. I would be entering the fifth grade. Even though I was still feeling pangs of guilt about some of the things we had done to other creatures, I was up for another adventure—and this one sounded a bit more challenging. It was looking to be a good morning.

"I was there the other day," Earl said as we started walking away from my house and down the gravel road. "There's tons of birds and squirrels in the pine trees. I think if you could push me up to a branch, I probably could get at the nests where they are and I could get some eggs or something. Or maybe we could find a squirrel nest."

"Really?" I asked. "That would be really neat to have a baby bird—or if I could keep a squirrel. But I dunno if Mumma would let me."

It was mid-morning as we walked up the hill to the woods. Earl's blonde-white hair—a towhead my mother called him—reflected the sun. With his tall, lanky stride, bib overalls and tee shirt, he looked like the Dennis the Menace kid on television.

"Ya gotta be quiet," he said to me even though I had not said anything at this point. As we started walking into the woods, Earl pulled out a large pocket knife and began looking for a small, sturdy stick.

"Whadya doing?" I asked.

"We need something to stick it with?" he answered.

"What are we gonna stick?"

"The squirrel," he said. "This is gonna be neat," he continued. "Just watch . . . ."

"Why are we gonna stick a squirrel?" I asked. "I thought we were gonna get one to keep."

Earl's mind had been racing faster than his words could come out. He had seen a squirrel climbing into the hole of a hollow tree. And with that, he had already devised a plan.

As he spoke, he quickly whittled a small piece of sassafras wood into a sharp spear. Then after we walked a little further, he pressed his ear firmly against a tree. "This is the one," Earl said. "You can hear 'em inside." He backed away from the tree and motioned for me to take a listen. For a moment, I held my breath—trying to become as quiet as I could.

"I don't hear anything," I said.

"Plug your other ear."

I stuck my finger in one ear and listened with the other—and there it was: a clawing and scratching on the other side of the wood that sounded like rats inside a wall.

"I hear 'em," I shouted.

"Move," he said pushing me aside. Earl began digging into the wood with his pocket knife. Methodically—as if he had done it a dozen times before—he sliced off pieces of the bark as if he were whittling the entire tree. After several moments, his shaving turned into gouging—almost as if he were trying to dig a splinter out of the tree. Finally, after fifteen or twenty minutes of shaving, gouging and digging, a hole appeared—and pushing through that hole was gray fur.

"That's it, that's it," he screamed. "I got it."

"Whadya gonna do?" I asked.

"I wanna make the hole bigger first," he said as he continued to dig. "I wanna be able to see it more."

As he drove his knife into the wood, the squirrel now began to squeal and screech—clawing wildly at the tree from the inside. Why it didn't escape, I didn't know. Maybe it was stuck or maybe it just didn't know how to get out.

The hole was now about as big as a half-dollar. We could easily see the squirrel moving around in a frantic frenzy.

"Look," Earl said, "it's got tits."

"Whadya mean? Where?"

"Right there," he said pointing to the squirrel's stomach. "That means she's got babies in there."

"Maybe we ought to leave her alone."

"Come on, Randy," he said. "We can get it."

I didn't say a thing as Earl continued to look intently at the squirrel. Her screeches and barks could be heard echoing through the surrounding woods. Earl picked up the stick he had whittled earlier and began poking at the squirrel—agitating her as much as he could. Each time he poked, she bit and clawed at the stick, trying to avoid the attack while not wanting to leave her babies. Within a moment or two, Earl's pokes became jabs. Small streams of blood started to trickle out of the wounds around her nipples. The squirrel screamed even louder—now moving around in the hole in a feverish panic. Earl and I both stood there—our gazes fixed on the work of his hands. The squirrel seemed to stare back at us desperately.

"If I kill it, we can get it out and eat it," he said still staring at the blood coming out of the squirrel.

"I don't want it," I answered. "I don't like squirrel."

"You ever had it?" he asked.

"Uh, uh," I said, shaking my head. "But I know I don't want any."

"Well, I'm gonna get it."

Earl now leveled the sharpened stick directly at the squirrel as she continued to squirm around in the tree. He pushed slowly so as to pin her against the other side—then, with one slow grinding motion, he plunged the stake through her. The squirrel cried and jerked—not wanting to give up. But after a moment, she was dead. We both stood there—not moving. The battle was over. The only noise was the slight whimper of the mother's litter as they moved around in the nest beneath her.

Earl took out his knife again and continued working to open the hole in the tree so as to retrieve the dead squirrel. But after digging for only a few seconds, he stopped.

"Oh, well," he said. "I don't reckon I can git it out anyway. It's too big." And with that, we left the woods.

For the rest of the morning, we wandered around the banks of Gagnon's pond—watching the snakes slither in and out of the water. Whenever we would happen upon bullfrogs that were just a little too slow, Earl liked to grab them, pick them up with a wide hand across their back and slam them stomach-first against a tree. The object of the exercise was to see how far you could make the guts splatter.

After executing a couple of frogs, Earl got an idea that we both thought was an incredible piece of imagination.

"Git that frog," he said, pointing to the remains of the one we had just killed. I picked up the green and red remains and handed it to him. He laid it on the ground and squatted next to the pier that stretched out into a shallow end of the pond. With his fingers like pinchers, he tore the skin that held on one of the hind legs. With delicate movements he plucked one hind leg off of the carcass. Hanging and dangling in the tree that hung over the pier was an assortment of old fishing bobbers and line that had been snagged by would-be fisherman. Earl stood up and reached up to the lowest branch and pulled down one of the bobbers with a piece of fishing line attached to it. Stretching it out between his hands, he bit down on the line to cut a piece about two feet long. Once he had his line, he squatted back down and tied the detached frog leg to the end of the line.

"We are gonna catch an eel," Earl said smiling.

I watched as he walked out to the end of the pier and tied the line to one of the wooden slats.

"How long before the eel comes?" I asked.

"Watch," he said.

Within a minute, we could see the fin of a long, gray eel swimming in the cloud of blood that was oozing from the dangling frog leg. At first, it nibbled—then it gulped the leg in one quick swallow.

As it did, Earl—still hunkered down at the end of the pier—reached into the water with both hands and grabbed the wriggling eel. Losing his balance, he fell forward as his elbows came to rest on the slats. The eel continued to wriggle as he squeezed it tighter and tighter. Gradually, Earl pushed himself up and onto his knees. Standing up with the eel in his hands, we were both once again caught in the excitement of the moment.

The eel began to hiss and squirm wildly as we stood there looking at it. Earl was getting tired of the fight so, holding it firmly, he swung it into a tree—like a baseball player swinging at a fastball. For the moment, the eel stopped its wild wriggling and we began our trek back to Earl's house.

By the time we reached the back porch, the eel was again hissing and squirming. Earl was laughing but I wasn't sure why. Yes, it was funny, but I wasn't sure if there was something else I was missing. Earl was thinking about the coming attractions.

He threw the eel down on the porch—but since it was dry ground, it wasn't going anywhere. I watched it squirm and wriggle and hiss a deep guttural sound while Earl ran inside to get something. After an instant, he came back with a small package in his hand.

"What is it?" I asked.

"They're fire crackers," he said. "My daddy got 'em when he was down in Galax. I was saving them for the Fourth of July, but this is gonna be a lot better."

As the eel continued to flop and move, Earl unwrapped the string of firecrackers. He handed them to me and told me to hold them. Then he reached down and picked up the eel and held it as it dangled and wiggled with its head looking up to the sky. He slid his hand up the back of the eel's head and squeezed the jaws to make the creature open its mouth.

"Git the fire crackers," he directed "Put 'em in his mouth—but don't drop 'em all the way in. Ya gotta light 'em first."

I looked at him for a moment—not saying a word and unsure if I could do what he asked. I bent over and opened the small box of wooden matches that were lying on the ground. Carefully, I slid it open and pulled out a match. I picked up the firecrackers and held them. Striking the match, I held it in one hand and the firecrackers with the other. Earl lowered the eel down so that I could place the firecrackers in its mouth. The eel slithered and squirmed as Earl held it more tightly. As I placed the firecrackers in the eel's mouth as far as I could, I lit the fuse. Earl quickly threw the eel to the far side of the porch. Within a second, the most horrific and strangest sound of muted pops and bangs, thuds and whumpfs came from inside of the slithering creature. It hissed and moaned its deep guttural voice as sparks, blue smoke and confetti-like paper came shooting out of its mouth and gills. And as fast as it had begun—the excitement came to an end. The eel lay motionless on the porch floor. The slithering, squirming and jerking had given way to a stillness only death could bring. The stench of burning eel was filling the air. Earl now grew anxious to get it off of the porch before his mother came out to see what carnage we had wrought.

Earl picked up the eel and threw its carcass into the woods nearby. During the next few days— whenever we walked near the spot where he had tossed the remains—we could smell the rotting flesh. But neither of us said anything about it—or even mentioned it in passing. We didn't speak about the squirrel or the eel—or any of the other horrible things we did. And just as my family never spoke about the things that had happened in our house—Earl never spoke about the beatings he received from his father. In looking back, I suppose killing squirrels, frogs, eels or whatever other animal we could find was our way of taking control over the things in our life that we could. It was our way of not always being victims. Earl had suffered at the hands of his daddy. My brothers and I had gotten more than our share from Jackson. The abomination of life with my father and perverted Scouts—and every other injustice— demanded that just as we had become victims, we now assert our power whenever and wherever we could. Even if it was over those who were too much like us.

Part Eight

Across the room was my father's second wife,
Jolene. Jolene Dotson was a teenager when she met
my father in 1964. Daddy's job had taken him to a
small telephone switching station in rural
Spotsylvania County where he installed wiring that
would provide some of the local farmers with modern
telephone systems—without local operators and party
lines. It was the kind of work he was good at and did a
lot of. How my father and Jolene first met or where
they first saw one another, I never knew. Eventually,
though, I heard stories of how Daddy's dark, slicked-
back hair and rugged features had swept the young
girl off her feet and into the arms of the handsome
man who worked for the phone company. Away from
our home in Mechanicsville for a week at a time, it
was easy for Daddy to meet girls like Jolene and to

live an alternate life. After all, it was nothing new. He had seen his father manage it quite well.

In the summer of 1964, Daddy took Jolene to the Spotsylvania County Fair. They spent the evening swooning together, playing games and riding the Ferris wheel. They even sat together in a small photo booth and had their picture taken. My old man was in his mid-thirties. Jolene was sixteen.

On weekends, Daddy would make the trek home—no matter where in Virginia his work had taken him. I guess in many ways, it provided him with a belief that there was some normalcy to his life—an illusion with which he deceived himself as well as others. Even though the work in Spotsylvania had been complete in a few months' time, he still managed to meet the teenager on a regular basis—for dates, outings with her parents, brothers and sisters—and obviously for sex. With an older man from Richmond taking such a special interest in her, the girl from Virginia's backwoods could not help but fall in love. She wanted to spend the rest of her life with Jackson. So it wasn't too big a deal when she discovered that she was pregnant. Jackson would marry her, she told herself, and life would go on. But she never knew that my father already had a family.

When Daddy heard that Jolene was pregnant, my father panicked. He stopped making his regular visits to Spotsylvania. He tried hiding in whatever way he could. Jolene's family hired a private investigator to find the man who had deflowered their little girl and then skipped town. Daddy finally told my mother about Jolene and about the baby girl who had now been born.

"Tell her we'll raise the baby," was my mother's response. "I'll raise her as my own. I always wanted a baby girl." Daddy wasn't buying that idea. He said that if he stayed out of sight, the Dotsons would never find him.

One morning, a middle-aged man in a gray suit knocked on the front door of our house on Roosevelt Avenue in Mechanicsville. It was funny that they called it an "avenue" because in those days it was just a dirt road covered with loose gravel. The stranger at the door told my mother he was selling life insurance and asked if he could come in and show her some of the plans his company offered. This was the early 1960s—long before people suspected the worst of one another. And this was Mechanicsville, a rural community in Virginia where neighbors knew one another, perhaps too well, and everyone was friendly. So without much hesitation, my mother let the man in. As I played on the floor in my bedroom with toy cars and a fuzzy teddy bear with a rubber face, my mother and the gentleman sat on the couch and flipped through page after page of insurance plans. As the man spoke, his eyes panned the room. He took in each photograph, asking rather specific details about each person in the picture. After a short time, the gentleman decided it was time to leave—saying that he would give my mother a few days to talk with my father so as to consider the various insurance plans. He never returned.

A few weeks later, Daddy received a summons from the sheriff's department. The Dotson's private investigator had been successful in finding my father and even in verifying his permanent residence. Daddy was sued for paternity.

"That man who came to sell you insurance," my father screamed at my mother. "He wasn't an insurance man. He was a goddamn private eye. He saw the pictures of me when he was here. That's how they found me. Goddamn it, Agnes. It's your goddamn fault this is happening. You should've hid those pictures—put 'em away somewhere. Goddamn it, Agnes."

It wasn't long afterward that Daddy and Mumma made the decision to separate. Maybe my father was hoping to start anew—to create a life better than the one he had built with our family in Mechanicsville. Or perhaps it was a decision of economics, deciding to support his teenage bride and one child instead of my mother, my brothers and me. Or it could have been that the idea of having a teenage beauty queen as a wife (Jolene had won a beauty prize at the Spotsylvania County Fair) appealed more to his fantasy. Whatever his reasoning, my father moved out of our house and didn't come back.

With Daddy gone, Mumma, my brothers and I struggled to get by. Cream-O-Wheat became the staple for breakfast and ketchup on white bread was standard fare in the middle of the day. Supper was hit or miss. Sometimes it was fried boloney; other times, tomato sandwiches or navy bean soup—but not both.

Our prayer life got better, though. When Carter, Jack, and I were out playing, we would pray that one of our friends would invite us to stay for the evening meal. What money did come in to our house was usually given to Mumma by her brothers and occasionally—unknown to Big Papa—her mother.

To get to the grocery store in town, my mother would either borrow an old car from one of our neighbors, or she would hoof it with one of us in tow to help carry the bags. Utility bills didn't get paid until something had already been shut off. Most weeks our telephone didn't work because Mumma couldn't afford to pay the bill. By the time I was ten years old, I knew how to turn the water back on after it had been shut off. The most exciting thing, though—actually, it could be quite terrifying—was restoring electricity to the house after the power company had come to turn it off.

At one point, two full days and two nights had passed since the electric company had disconnected us. Neighborhood kids and their parents had started to ask what was going on and had even taken to mocking the "poor old Jordans." Mumma, humiliated at the level of our poverty, told my brothers and me to look around the house and find as many candles as we could. As the sun set on the third day, she closed the Venetian blinds and placed several of the luminaries in front of each window. The effect was to make it seem like the Jordans had electricity, that whatever oddness taking place had passed. Very early on the third morning, Carter told me to follow him outside.

He wanted me to learn how to do what our daddy had taught him to do.

"You watch but don't touch anything," my brother warned.

We walked over to the electric meter hanging on the side of the house, just below where the power lines connected near the roof. Carefully, Carter took the pair of wire cutters he had brought outside with us and clipped a "tamper seal" hanging on the metal ring that wrapped around the meter.

"You have to clip it real close to the edge so the electric man can't see where you cut it," he instructed. After cutting the tamper seal, Carter uncoupled the metal ring and pulled it from around the meter. Then, with both hands, he pulled the meter from its base and set it on the ground. Behind the meter were two prongs sticking out from the base of the meter—like the prongs on the plug of a giant electric cord.

"This is where ya gotta be real careful," he said. "Daddy said if ya touch 'em, it'll kill you. Fry ya like a piece 'a bacon." With the finesse of a surgeon, my brother delicately removed the rubber booties that had been covering the prongs. He breathed a slight sigh of relief and then placed the booties in his pocket. He then re-assembled the meter and replaced the tamper seal, bending the wire, making it appear that no one had cut it.

"That's what ya do," he said proudly.

We walked back into the house. We had electricity. Unfortunately, it was to be a skill my brothers and I would have to use on more than one occasion.

Not long after Daddy moved out, he and Jolene stood before a justice of the peace at the Spotsylvania County Courthouse and were married. It would be decades before Jolene would discover that her marriage to my father was invalid, because he was still married to my mother at the time. Nevertheless, she and Daddy lived as husband and wife.

Daddy, Jolene and their new baby, Renee, eventually made their home in a trailer park in Lakeside, just outside of Richmond. During their time together, Jolene would have five more children in what seemed to be a single pregnancy which lasted more than a decade. In a matter of just a short time, though, my father's dark side grew even darker as he and his other family now lived like rats packed in a tin box. As the demons of his youth clung tightly to his emotions, Daddy's vicious abuse continued. Just as in our house, dishes were routinely smashed. Children were regularly whipped with sticks, belts, and electric cords. Daughters were slapped, had their hair yanked and buttocks smacked with various instruments. Boys could be punched or choked at any time. Jolene— once the winner of teenage beauty pageants—was now grossly overweight and in poor health. She also had bruises of her own. Even though my father ate well, his "other children" survived on the scraps he threw to them. Drunken tirades opened the doors to cruel, vile tongue-lashings that could be intertwined with any number of physical threats. The police were regularly called and on more than one occasion, Daddy stayed in jail just long enough to sober-up. But when he returned home the next morning, he always got his revenge.

In October 1986, things finally changed. At five-thirty in the afternoon, just as he had for so many years, my father returned home at the end of a work day. But he didn't find a wife busy in the kitchen. There were no children anxiously performing their daily chores. My father came home to emptiness. An empty kitchen, empty bedrooms, and an empty life. Jolene and all of her children were gone.

Over the course of nearly a year, Jolene had taken a little bit of money from the grocery allowance my father had doled out to her and hidden it away. She had also convinced Daddy that in order for the family to continue to make ends meet, she should work a part-time job at the Seven-Eleven just around the corner. Daddy had agreed, and Jolene had lied about her salary. Secretly, she had established her own checking account and had charged small purchases so as to create a credit history. And on an October morning in 1986—after her husband had left for work, she hurriedly packed everything she could and moved out. She and her children had escaped my father.

As bizarre as it seemed to me, Jolene never did cut ties completely with Daddy. In his final year of life, as he lay bed-ridden from advanced heart disease and cancer, she visited him three times a week— mainly to wash his clothes and do some light housecleaning. She charged him $300 a week.

I continued to gaze around the parlor. There were the faces of my father's "other children." Thomas, the oldest son of Daddy's other family, was the one I had known best. In too many ways his face resembled that of our father's. And like Jack, Thomas, too, had received more than his share of attention.

Carter, Jack, and I never wanted to visit our father after our parents had separated. Even though the trailer park where Daddy lived was not that far away, Mumma assured us that if we did not go to visit our daddy, any financial support she might randomly receive from him would disappear completely. So every month or so, off we went.

A visit to Daddy's was never pleasant. It was a true test of nerves. But some visits were more unbearable than others. There were tell-tale signs my brothers and I looked for that told us if a visit would be tolerable or not. They mostly had to do with smells. Whenever I walked into his trailer, I could always smell either stale beer or coffee. If I smelled coffee, it would be a tolerable meeting. He wouldn't be drunk. And if he wasn't drunk, I wouldn't hear the cursing, swearing, and tales of family injustice that were trademarks of visits with my father. If I smelled stale beer, there would be trouble.

I had always hoped to someday discover a way to find out what the smell would be without having to tip my father off that I had come to visit. I wanted to figure out some way to find out if it was going to be coffee or beer—without having to open the door. But I never did. And on this particular night it was beer.

It had been a few weeks since I had last seen Daddy. And during that time, Thomas had begun to grow facial hair. In the near month since my last visit, his upper lip had grown a hefty amount of brown fuzz.

When I came through my father's front door, I knew what kind of visit it was going to be. But once I had committed to coming through the door, there was no turning back. I walked over to give Daddy the expected kiss on the cheek. As I sat on the couch across from my father, Thomas came in to the living room to say hello. Jolene offered me a Pepsi-Cola. As she walked over to the refrigerator and filled two large glasses with ice, my father sat there smiling.

"Jolene," my father yelled to his wife, "gimme some more ice and another beer." My father always poured his beer into an ice-filled glass.

"Yes sir," she answered.

"Hey boy," he said looking over to me. "Where ya been?"

"Workin'," I answered, searching for a reason for not having come to visit sooner. "I've been working a lot. Just about every day after school."

"Where ya workin'?"

"At Doctor Thompson's drugstore."

This idle talk filled the next few minutes. My father used these moments to prepare the assault he would launch on an unsuspecting victim. During my teen years, I had seen him slice and dice his way through friends, family, and total strangers. His children were his easiest prey. Jolene brought us our drinks and then went to the back of the trailer.

"Hey," my father said looking at Thomas. "What's on your lip?"

"It's my moustache," Thomas answered proudly, stroking the hair with his index finger and thumb.

We each chuckled a little—enjoying light conversation, but neither of us was prepared for what came next.

"It looks good. I think it looks pretty," he said measuring his slurred words. "Hey," Daddy said as he moved his hands down to his crotch. "if ya pulled out your teeth, your mouth would feel just like a pussy." His vulgarity paralyzed and shocked us. "Come on, boy. Whadya say you suck my dick?"

Thomas sat silently—staring at my father. His eyes filled with tears and his lower jaw quivered as he began to cry. At the other end of the couch, I sat still—afraid to make any movement that might call attention to my presence. I was horrified, but my horror quickly turned to fear. My father looked at me—encouraging me to laugh. I was afraid that his cruelty would stab into me. I worked a smile, but I could only sit and watch Thomas. I should have said something, but I was scared and said nothing.

All these many years later, as he stood in the parlor, Thomas now looked even more like our father. His face had grown the same lines as Daddy's, the same tilt of his eyes gave a near-constant expression of sadness to his smile. I supposed it had grown that way through the years.

Part Nine

As the evening grew on, the funeral parlor grew more and more crowded with uncles, aunts, old neighbors, cousins, and friends I had not seen in more than thirty years. Peppered here and there were those faces totally unfamiliar to me, perhaps relatives, possibly friends I had forgotten or simply did not want to remember. No matter how many I saw, though, what returned to my mind was the anguish many of us had endured at the hands of our fathers.

After living on the farm for just a few years, my mother moved us to a house in one of Mechanicsville's small, rural neighborhoods—which was merely a collection of few houses spread out near the intersection of a couple of out-of-the-way tarred roads. For Carter, Jack, and me, the move meant we had more opportunities to interact with other kids. It was a welcome change.

By now, Carter was seventeen and had started driving. He had earned enough money working on Bland Sledd's farm after school to buy an old Karmann Ghia. The car ran when Carter bought it. After a month or so he decided to try to rebuild the engine himself, so as to make it run better. Within a few weeks of pulling the car apart, though, he discovered that getting it back together again wasn't going to be easy. From then on, the unassembled car sat in the garage of our rented house. He eventually sold the parts and used his thumb for transportation. Hitchhiking whenever he needed to go somewhere. As for my middle brother, Mumma had decided that Jack was unmanageable, to use her words. So—without my father's knowledge—she sent him to live with my aunt and uncle in Michigan for a year. There, he got to watch my uncle beat my cousins. At least Jack didn't get beaten during the year or so he lived with them. For my part, I made friends with guys who had the same axes to grind that I did—boys who had been beaten by their fathers and silently seduced by their mothers. They weren't hard to find.

Of all my friends, one of those who fascinated me the most was a boy named John Tomkins. Johnny, as he was still called back then, was a year older than me, with a head of sandy-blonde hair and a fair complexion that never seemed to tan during the summer months. It only turned red. Like so many of us at that time, in that place and in that life, Johnny had a fascination with hunting relics left over from the War Between the States. Hanover County had been the sight of so many historic battles: Cold Harbor, Gaines Mill, The Seven Days, and so on. The woods where we played and built forts were filled with buttons, buckles, badges, and bullets just waiting to be unearthed from under a thin layer of topsoil. In the fall, nearly each day after school, a number of us would borrow a metal detector from anyone who owned one and begin digging in some field where a battle was known to have taken place, or in mounds of dirt created by the building of earthworks and other fortifications a century before—desperately searching for a treasure to be placed in a box and not-soon forgotten. But Johnny didn't dig in fields. He had a much different tactic.

In his few years of relic-hunting, Johnny Tomkins had amassed quite a trove of nineteenth century valuables and even an occasional eighteenth century discovery. The mere thought of his methods for acquiring the pieces, though, was too depraved for any of the rest of us to even consider. While the sun was high in the sky, Johnny would wander through old family cemeteries—graveyards long forgotten and perhaps even abandoned, left to become overgrown with weeds and vines. Methodically, he would note the dates carved in the stone tablets placed at the head of the deceased who lay six feet beneath the earth. Just to make sure he could find the grave again, he would place a few rocks on the top of those tombstones which identified the deceased as a soldier or someone of earthly importance. And on a warm moonlit night, Johnny Tomkins would return to the hallowed ground to dig.

"It really dudn't take that long," Johnny once explained. "Most times, it's really not six feet. Sometimes it's four or five. If it's too deep, I'll come back a night or two later 'n finish. Nobody cares about 'em anyway. They're just graves that people have forgot about."

Each season, Johnny took care not to rob too many graves at any one time. He wanted to make sure that—if anyone suspected anything—they would see it as an occasional act of vandalism, not a pattern of theft. But while his bounty included swords, buckles, brooches, watches and an assortment of jewelry, he seemed to derive a most unusual pleasure in smashing the skulls of those he had unearthed. "It's jus' a lotta fun!" he would whisper.

One afternoon after school, one of the boys from my new neighborhood, Berkley—Lee, as he goes by now—and I were passing through a copse of trees. We were on our way to Timberlake's pond. A few days earlier while he was fishing, Berkley had seen a large wasp nest hanging over the pond from the branch of a tree on the bank. The discovery meant an afternoon of using our slingshots to whack the nest and watch the wasps fall into the pond. As the wasps fell from the nests, they would swirl in the water—which would attract the fish. The fish would then eat the wasps, and we could only imagine what the fish must have been thinking after eating a swarm of angry wasps.

As we followed the path to the pond, we passed the Eppers family cemetery, a small plot of ground about thirty feet square. The last Eppers' family member had died sometime in the 1940s, so no one ever came there anymore. Well off the beaten path and surrounded by a four foot high brick wall, it had been the perfect place to hide during the war games we always played.

As we walked past the graveyard, just as we had done dozens of times before, my friend and I looked at the old tombstones. But for the first time ever, we noticed a large, recently-dug hole—about five feet long and three feet wide—near the center of the cemetery.

"Looks like Johnny's been digging," Berkley said with a slight laugh.

"I always wondered if those stories were true," I said.

"Now ya know," Berkley answered.

"It would be kind 'a neat to hide somewhere and scare the shit outta him when he comes back," I said.

"He won't be back tonight," Berkley said. "The moon won't be out again for a few nights. It's gonna be too dark to dig."

Standing in the graveyard, we continued looking around—noticing the stone tablets and commenting on the scariness of the scene.

"We should bring Peewee here," I said.

"Whadya mean?" Berkley asked.

"I could tell him I found something neat in the cemetery and wanted him to see it too," I explained. "He's dumb as dirt. He won't think twice about it. Then," I continued, "you could get in the hole and start making moaning noises right after we climb over the wall."

For the next few minutes, Berkley and I stood in the graveyard, looking in the half-dug hole Johnny had started the night before. "I ain't climbing in that hole. Let's wait 'til dark and then you bring him here. I'll hide behind one of the gravestones and make noises." Mulling over our plans, we decided that the wasp nest could wait another day.

As we walked back home, we decided that for the desired effect, props would be needed. Berkley got one of his daddy's old jackets and a wig that his mother used "on special occasions." I contributed a bone our dog had been gnawing on for a week or so, a bunch of old newspapers and a bottle of ketchup. Berkley also got a road flare from under the seat of his daddy's truck. With materials in hand, and daylight quickly passing, we ran back to the graveyard and created our scene.

Despite the number of houses in our small neighborhood, there really weren't that many kids to hang out with. But of the few who did hang around with Berkley and me, there was one kid in particular I really did not like. His name was Peewee Reddington. It wouldn't be accurate to say I hated the boy. After all, I knew it wasn't right to hate somebody, no matter what they did, but it seemed I couldn't help disliking

Peewee. He was a smelly, know-it-all kid with black, greasy hair, and even though he had not yet reached eleven years old, he had already begun cussing like a sailor and chewing tobacco. His teeth—already stained from the brown leaves he sucked on—had begun to rot.

He was new to the neighborhood—newer than me. His family had just moved in from West Virginia. Like anyone else, I suppose, he desperately wanted to be accepted, in this case by my friends and me—the older boys—but I was going to make sure he traveled a hard road to get it.

As the sun set, I walked toward the Reddingtons' house. Peewee had been outside playing with his little brother. They were both getting ready to head inside for supper.

"Hey, Peewee!" I yelled hoping to stop him before he got inside his house.

"Hey-hey, Jordan," he stammered back. I hated that he always called me by my last name. His stammering was also something I didn't like.

"I found something down near Timberlake's pond," I said. "Me 'n Berkley thought maybe you and Turtle would wanna see it—but if ya gotta go eat, then maybe tomorrow."

"I ain't going," Peewee's little brother, Turtle, said without taking any time to consider the invitation. In reality, it wasn't that Turtle, whose real name was Jody, didn't want to see whatever it was we might have found; he just didn't trust me. A few weeks earlier, Berkley and I had used the boy for target practice. It all started as he passed in front of my house while walking down the tarred road. Seeing the little boy, we yelled to him to wait up—that we wanted to show him something. While Turtle stood out by the road, Berkley and I went into my garage and filled glass Christmas ornaments with dirt. Mumma had thought our Christmas decorations would be safer there than in the attic where it got so hot during the summer. After filling a few glass Christmas balls half-way with dirt, I then went into a corner, turned my back to Berkley and peed in each of them, providing just enough urine to fill each of them up the rest of the way. Then I placed the metal clip back in the hole where the hangers usually attach and gently set them right side up in the ornament box. We treated the box of pee-mud ornaments as carefully as a soldier would a box of hand grenades.

As Turtle stood out by the road, Berkley yelled to the little boy, "Here catch!" and we began throwing the glass balls at the kid. Realizing that he was being ambushed, the little boy started running down the road toward his house. At first, Berkley and I both missed our target completely. But just before the kid had reached the outer limits of my throwing range—a shiny, red, glass, urine-and-mud-filled Christmas ornament smacked Turtle squarely on the crown of his head. The poor boy let out a heart wrenching scream and cried the rest of the way back to his house. Our encounter this particular afternoon was the first time I had seen him since then.

"N-n-no—I can come," Peewee answered pushing his little brother aside. Peewee ran towards me as I continued walking down the road. Running to catch up with me, he began asking questions in a breathless stammer.

"Wh-wha-what did ya find?" he asked.

"You won't believe it," I answered.

"What is it?" he asked again.

"It's so cool . . . you just won't believe it. You're gonna have to see it yourself."

As we continued walking, I slowed our pace, wanting to make sure darkness had had a chance to set in before we reached the graveyard. Finally, we veered off the gravel road and hiked across a broad field that led to the edge of the woods where the path toward the pond began. Once we reached the path, it would only be a matter of a few yards before we reached the cemetery. By now, it was just beginning to get dark.

"Th-th-this is the place I-I-I hate most," he said—his stammering now worsening. "I-I hate walking pass th-th' grave yard."

"Don't be a chicken, Peewee," I said as we stepped off the path and toward the brick wall. Eager to prove his mettle, he followed close behind me. I raised my voice slightly as we peered over the wall.

"It's just a grave yard." With that cue, a deathly moan rose eerily from the darkness. At the same time, a red glow burst from behind one of the large tombstones, draping the entire scene in a pale red hue. There, in the middle of the ground before us lay a human figure wearing an old coat—face-down in the dirt. From its sleeve stretched a boney, blood-soaked arm . . . reaching for something, anything, to pull itself from the netherworld—desperately clawing its way from Johnny Tomkins' freshly dug grave.

I had planned to scream something like, "Oh shit," but before I could get the words out of my mouth, Peewee was already running down the path that led back to the field and out to the gravel road. His screams and whimpers could be heard fading into the distance. We later learned from his younger brother that Peewee had arrived home terrified and shaking, his pants wet with fear. Berkley and I laughed hard that night, harder than I would in the weeks, months, and years to follow.

Part Ten

So many of those in the parlor knew all too well the toll our childhood had taken on our adult lives. While light conversation and gentle reminiscences protected us from the pain of our memories—even if just for an evening, deeper feelings covered the room. Looking at the faces of those I could remember, I knew their stories. Occasionally, though, there were the faces of those who had taken up the mantle of abuse themselves. Boys I had known as playmates who even while they were children had already moved into another realm of power and domination.

Long before I had disliked Peewee Reddington, there had been a boy who I truly did learn to hate. Even though Mumma would always correct me and say, "No, you don't hate him—you dislike him," I knew that in reality, I hated him. His name was Sonny Blake.

The Blake family lived across the road from us when we lived on Roosevelt Avenue. Except for their house, all of the houses on our short road—including ours—were constructed of cement blocks and painted white. The houses had been built for those soldiers returning home after the Second World War and moving from the city into what would eventually be called the "suburbs." The Blakes' house, though, was bigger—with three bedrooms instead of two. They also had two toilets in their house.

I really don't know when I first met Sonny Blake. Our cement-block house was the first home I had ever known and Sonny had lived across the road for as long as I could remember. My earliest remembrance of him, though, is that he was an okay kid. Like most of us back then, he had a dog. The dog's name was Pat which I thought was a rather peculiar name for an animal. The neat thing about Sonny's house, though—besides having two bathrooms inside—was that getting there meant turning off of our gravel road and walking down a narrow dirt lane that ran a short ways into woods filled with pine trees. Their dirt lane was shaded with persimmon trees which bore an abundance of fruit every summer, so walking to his house meant eating as many persimmons as my stomach could hold.

After arriving at Sonny's house, we usually spent time blowing up plastic army men with firecrackers, or shooting them off of stumps with BB guns. Sonny also had a trick he liked to perform with Pat. He would grab the dog and pull her to him. Then he would wrap his arms around the back part of her mid-section—near her butt—and squeeze her until she farted. The very first time he did it, it was funny. But he did it several times a day, every day. I supposed we still laughed, just not as much. For a long time, it seemed that Sonny was just like the rest of us, but eventually he seemed to develop a little twist. He was with us when we built dams in the creeks and scavenged for crayfish. He was with us when we went to experience the wonderment of flying squirrels—amazed as they glided from one tree to another. He was also with us whenever we went hunting for snakes or bullfrogs at Gagnon's pond. But the "twist" that made Sonny different was his insatiable desire to take things too far. When we killed an animal for fun—such as a crayfish or a toad—Sonny was the one who would want to find something to do with the entrails, such as burning them and watching them pop or just lighting a match under something dead long enough to see what it smelled like. It was entertaining at first, but after a while even the hardiest of us was grossed out.

Just up the gravel road from Sonny's house—past my house, across the creek and up the hill a ways—

was where Little Tom lived, the kid who we had renamed because he shared the same name as my middle brother. Little Tom was a nice boy, but even though he was nice didn't mean he was always invited to play with us. The reason usually given for his exclusion was because he was too little. But there was also another reason; the boy had a tendency to steal stuff. Once, he stole Mrs. Blake's wedding ring off the window sill over her kitchen sink. She had taken it off to do dishes and after Little Tom had gone in the house to use the bathroom, the ring was missing. Mrs. Blake came out to ask if anyone had seen her ring. Since Little Tom was the only one who had gone in the house, Sonny started cursing at him. Mrs. Blake didn't seem to mind. Then he chased Little Tom down the dirt road, all the while cussing at him for stealing it. Little Tom was the faster runner, but once he got far enough ahead, he stopped. He bent over to tie his shoe and then as he stood back up, he held up Mrs. Blake's ring.

"Look!" Little Tom said. "I found this right here. Is this your mumma's ring?"

He wasn't allowed over the Blakes' house for a long time after that—unless Cathy was with him.

Cathy was Little Tom's twin sister. Whenever Little Tom was invited to play with us, it was usually because we all wanted to see Cathy. Even though she had just turned eleven years old, Cathy Grubbs was prettier than any girl we knew—especially in the summertime. The blonde hair that fell to her shoulders turned even blonder in the sun, and her smooth skin had the same light tan as a loaf of fresh-baked bread, at least that's what I always thought it looked like. With green eyes and a laugh that made people laugh with her, she was the girl all the boys wanted to be around. But there was one thing that made her extra special—her voice. Even though her twin brother had the high-pitched squeak of a toddler, an annoying whine actually, Cathy's tone was more mature, a bit husky with a slight rasp. In so many ways, it made her beauty more complete.

During the fall, it was always easier and safer to build forts and hideouts in the woods near our houses. By late November, cold weather had gotten rid of most of the weeds and the pine trees had dropped their brown tags, creating a soft carpet beneath the trees. Cooler weather had also forced snakes, spiders and other pests into hibernation—so just before Thanksgiving, the woods were the place where we played most.

It was a chilly afternoon when Little Tom, Cathy, Sonny and I had started building our fort in the pine woods. We had been stacking large branches and pine tags beneath a thicket of honeysuckle vines for the better part of an hour or more since we had gotten home from school. As we were completing the roof, layering one pine branch on top of another, Little Tom reminded his sister that they were supposed to be home for supper by five o'clock. The sun had begun to get low in the sky when Little Tom announced he was leaving. He started down the path back to the gravel road.

"Come on, Cathy," Little Tom whined. "Mumma's gonna be mad if you are late 'n Daddy's gonna give you a whipping when he gets home from work."

"Go on," Cathy said. "I just wanna finish putting more branches on the roof."

As Sonny, Cathy and I finished our work, Little Tom ran down the path and within a moment he was out of sight.

"We can come back tomorrow," I said. Cathy and Sonny agreed and the three of us began making our way back to the road.

As we left the fort, I was quite a few steps ahead of Cathy. Sonny was following her at a close distance. As I made my way around a curve in the path, I heard a muffled sound behind me. I didn't think much of it at first, thinking that someone must've tripped or such. But after a moment, I could no longer see my friends. It was then that I heard Cathy shouting.

"Stop," her raspy voice commanded. At the same time, I could hear Sonny laughing. "Stop it, Sonny," she said again.

I turned around and walked the short distance back to see what was happening. As I made my way around the bend of the path, Cathy was lying face down on the ground, her pants pulled down to her knees. She was struggling to push herself off the ground, but Sonny was lying on top of her—his hand groping.

"Stop," she screamed again. Cathy struggled hard to wrestle out from beneath Sonny's body, all the while doing the best she could to keep her thighs pressed tightly together. I stood there for a second, shocked at what I was seeing. I knew what I was seeing wasn't right, but I also knew I wasn't supposed to see Cathy's nakedness. I turned my face away.

"Sstttoppp," she screamed even louder.

Sonny, appearing to have become engrossed in his own actions, suddenly looked up. Whether it was the surprise of my return, the fear of discovery, or the guilt of molesting Cathy—I did not know. But for some reason, Sonny stopped. After a second, he climbed off of Cathy, laughing as he did. Cathy—still unsure of what had just taken place—struggled to pull her pants up before getting to her feet. None of us said a word. Sonny pushed past me and headed home. Cathy wiped her face, brushed off her clothes and continued walking home as well. I, too, left the woods without words, overwhelmed at my own shame and embarrassment. The next day, the fort was finished. Cathy stayed home.

In the years since, I have often wondered what would have happened had I not gone back around the bend in the path. I wonder if Cathy was Sonny's first victim, or if she was his last. I have also thought about Cathy—her powerlessness, her loss—as she was fondled and groped by the boy lying on top of her. I wonder where she is now and if she has sons and daughters of her own. I wonder what she has taught them. I wonder what she does to manage the memories, what she does to keep her secrets.

Part Eleven

In the middle of the crowd stood an unfamiliar man wearing a clerical collar. While my brothers and I had grown up Catholic, there were few in the funeral parlor this night who still practiced it. My father's maternal grandfather had been the pastor of the Methodist Episcopal church on the corner of Twentieth and Broad streets on Church Hill—"the church that got struck by lightning," was the way Daddy identified the building. But the family holiness had not been passed on to my father. Nanny had married outside of her faith and attended church only once in a blue moon—and in Richmond the moon was seldom blue. Just before my father married my mother, Daddy had converted to Catholicism. Nanny remarked that she was sure her father was turning in his grave for it was far better to be un-churched than Catholic.

As people continued signing the condolence book and paying their respects, I noticed a couch in the middle of the parlor. It was one of those pieces of furniture that would only be found in a funeral home. It was quite formal, with claw feet and a camel back, but the whole thing was as stiff as my father's body. The placement of the sofa seemed rather odd to me— nearly hidden by a crowd of people standing throughout the room. But what I found even more peculiar was the fact that Mumma was sitting on it— my mother, the woman who had suffered so terribly at the hands of my father and who, after being divorced from him for more than forty years and not seeing him for more than twenty, would still tell anyone who would listen of the torment she had endured.

My mother had grown up in Richmond throughout the 1930s and 40s. There, she had spent what she described as the happy, carefree days of her youth. Only much later in her life, would she concede that those days had been neither happy nor carefree.

From the pictures I later saw of my mother in her childhood and teenage years, I know she was quite a handsome woman. Dark hair fell to her shoulders and she had kept fit by playing basketball at the Catholic school in Church Hill. She would always tell the story of how she had fouled out of the last game of her senior year. Even though she had sad eyes, all of her pictures showed a face filled with a smile that expressed joy and happiness. Much later in her life, that smile would still be there—but by then I knew that it hid a melancholy madness.

Neither my mother nor her only sister would ever speak in loving terms about their father. Whenever we went to visit my mother's parents, we would go without Daddy. He refused to go. Once we were there, Mumma would duck into the kitchen so as to spend more time with her mother than with her stern, sullen father.

Eddie Martin, Mumma's father, wasn't very tall. The nickname his grandchildren had given him had been more a reflection of his domineering nature than his physical stature. With white hair combed straight back, a thick nose and long, detached earlobes that resembled Lyndon Johnson's, he was anything but an attractive man. He always smelled of Old Spice and wine and whenever he smiled, empty spaces of decaying teeth filled his mouth. But despite his need for teeth—whenever a woman entered the room (a woman who wasn't related to him) my grandfather's face lit up. His broad smile made his fat lips curl over around his gums. For nearly all his life, he had prized himself as a lady's man—a misogynist actually. And the stories of his conquests—the women he had used and abused—were legendary. My grandmother, on the other hand, seemed to be the complete opposite of her husband. Quiet, loving, cordial and—as some would swear—a truly holy woman. Big Mama's family never approved of her marriage. Eddie was not a descendant of Virginia's first families. Why she married beneath her, as her family would always say, remained a lifelong mystery.

Big Mama was a small woman, barely five feet tall, with a rounded, rather long nose for a woman. Her hair had been dark when she was much younger, but by the time I knew her, it had turned a light brown with a little grey. As nearly all old people do, she wore glasses. The only kind I can really remember her ever wearing had light blue frames that came to a somewhat fashionable point at the sides. No other part of her wardrobe, though, ever appeared to be in style. Rather, her clothes were more second-hand, pass-me-downs from some well-meaning friend or relative.

My grandmother's family, the Anthonys, had been wealthy before the crash of '29. Big Mama's grandfather had gotten involved in tobacco and cotton after the War Between the States and by the mid-1880s had built a large, fashionable home on Main Street in Richmond. When Louise and Eddie got married, the money was still rolling in so much so that their wedding gift was a house in the city's up-and-coming neighborhood of Highland Park. By the 1930s, though, all that changed. Big Mama had given birth to eight children and Eddie, my grandfather, had become an abusive womanizer. Had they not owned their house, it is doubtful whether they would have been able to keep it during those years of turmoil.

In October of 1960, my grandmother had a massive heart attack. Doctors did not expect her to make it through the night so they summoned the entire family and advised them to say their goodbyes. My grandmother hung on, though—surviving the night and after more than three weeks in the hospital, she returned home. Another twenty six years later, her heart finally gave out.

After her heart attack, Big Mama could neither make the trip to her bedroom upstairs, nor was she able to care for the house the way she had done before. So the family hired a colored woman ("colored" was the respectful term, my mother would explain, for describing a person of African descent) and a colored person who worked in a white household, my mother would continue, was called a "domestic." My grandmother's domestic was Miss Maggie.

At that point in my brief life, I had only seen black people from a distance. I even paid a black boy a dime to shine my shoes one Saturday afternoon just so I could get a bit closer than usual. Miss Maggie was the first black person I had ever really known. Schools were segregated, so there were no black kids in my school. There were no black people in my church, none in the supermarket. I did see a black man working in the drugstore every now and then. But for the most part, like most white people back then, I never saw colored people. Not because they weren't there, but because they were invisible. We never saw them until they mattered.

Miss Maggie was tall, much taller than Big Mama. She was more light brown than black. The most memorable things about her, though, were the manner in which she spoke to and about people and the marvelous way in which she would include me in her conversations. She spoke with kindness and gentleness—never raising her voice nor showing any signs of becoming flustered, no matter how demanding my grandfather could be. And when she spoke about her husband, Benjamin, there was a sparkle in her eye, one which I would never forget and—in later years—recognize as a reflection of love emanating deep from within a tender heart.

"Whadya think I should do 'bout that, Randy?" she would say whenever something seemed to perplex her. It was her way of making even the smallest child feel a part of her world.

"Ma'am?" I would say in response—even with colored folks, Mumma and Daddy always made us say ma'am or sir.

Miss Maggie would laugh and ask me the same question again while she scrubbed clothes on the back porch or starched my grandfather's shirts in the kitchen.

It was a spring day when I happened to be at Big Mama's for lunch. School had let out early for some reason, so I walked down to my grandparents' house until Mumma could pick me up. Miss Maggie had fixed my grandmother a plate of fruit, cottage cheese and saltines with a glass of skim milk.

"What you want ta eat, Randy?" she asked.

I looked at her. No one had ever asked me what I wanted to eat. I had always been given food and told to eat it. As we stood in the kitchen, I stared at Miss Maggie, not really knowing what to say.

"Well," I said as I stretched out my thoughts, "what are you gonna eat?"

"I'm havin' a peanut butter 'n cheese samwich," Miss Maggie said.

"Peanut butter 'n cheese?" I asked. "That dudn' sound good. We eat peanut butter 'n mayonnaise . . . b' not peanut butter 'n cheese."

"You ever had it?" she asked.

"No, ma'am."

"Well then how do ya know you won' like it?"

I thought for a moment, staring at Miss Maggie. By this time, her face had spread into a broad smile and sporadic, gentle laughter had begun to fill the kitchen. In the end, we both enjoyed our peanut butter and cheese sandwiches with tall glasses of cold milk. The delight of that afternoon was not something I would forget. On more than one occasion as I rode with my mother to take Miss Maggie home, I asked if I could come in and stay with her. Mumma was always quick to say that we had to go—it was always "gettin' late." Years later, as an adult, I had always wanted to go look for Miss Maggie, to see where she had gone to or what had become of her. But she and her husband both had long passed away. As a stranger, she had taught me so much about kindness and the gentleness of grace. As a woman of African descent, she had taught me that it didn't matter what color I was. She would love me even if I wasn't black.

Out of all the things my mother could have changed in her life, it would have been her father. He rarely showed any affection to my mother and her sister. Even as an adult, whenever Mumma would walk over to him to give him a hug goodbye, he would push her away. Then, just as she would turn to walk away, his hand would come hard across her butt—hard enough that tears would well up in my mother's eyes. It was a scene that was repeated over and over again—whenever we left his house. I never understood why my mother kept going to him.

My mother's presence at my father's wake in many ways was just a confirmation of the denial which had so often been a part of her life. She had denied my father's habitual violence. She had denied his alcoholism. She had denied his infidelity—even to the point of offering to adopt his bastard child. And after my father left, Mumma would continue to live in denial. Refusing to believe that she must be a parent to three boys, she would—using her sons as partners—craft an art of silent seduction.

We were still living in the old farmhouse when Daddy finally stopped coming for his unannounced visits. He had chosen Jolene and it was clear to my mother that this was the end of their marriage. From that point on, it seemed, my mother began her quest of finding someone else who would save her from herself and her misery.

The week after Daddy announced that things were officially over between himself and my mother, Mumma made her first attempt at suicide. While it was a dramatic event, it really wasn't life-threatening. She had taken just enough sleeping pills to make sleep longer than usual. The next morning was a Saturday. Carter had already left for his job at Sledd's farm and Jack and I were sitting in the living room eating cereal. As we sat there, we could see Mumma slowly descending the stairs, still dressed in her night gown and duster, holding on to the banister with both hands. Her face was streaked with tears.

"Ya'll go call ya Uncle Junie," she said biting her lip. "Tell 'im I tried ta kill myself . . . that I took too many sleeping pills."

Jack called our uncle and within an hour, he had made the drive from Richmond through Mechanicsville and down the long dirt lane. Uncle Junie made some instant coffee for my mother and then spent some time talking with her upstairs. He told her she needed to see a psychiatrist. It was also about this time that Mumma began acting strangely towards Carter and me. Later, this strange behavior would be characterized by my psychiatrist as silent seduction.

On the first floor of our old farmhouse, there were two large rooms situated on either side of a staircase that was located in the middle of the house. The kitchen, a late nineteenth century addition, was located to the right of the back of the house. The second floor had the same layout as the first floor, except built over the kitchen was an extra bedroom.

At the top of the stairs, one had to turn to the left to go into the room that Jack and I shared. Carter's room was the smaller room over top the kitchen, so getting to Carter's room meant going through my and Jack's room. The other place to go at the top of the stairs—if not going into my and Jack's room—was the bathroom, which was directly in the middle of the house. This meant that in order to get to my mother's room, a person had to pass through the bathroom. It was a strange layout, but since all plumbing was outside when the house was built in the early 1800s, the bathroom had been a late addition as well.

Carter was sixteen years old when we lived on the farm. And despite the fact that our father had made our world tortuous, life went on. We ate. We slept. We went to school and our bodies continued to grow. We even fantasized about a better life and, of course, girls.

Most people know what nearly all boys have discovered about themselves by the time they are sixteen. Normal teenage boys know they have genitals and they have discovered that it doesn't take much stimulation before involuntary movement occurs. My oldest brother was a normal teenage boy.

It wasn't until much later in my life that I learned about boundaries, how parents will allow their children privacy and the space they need to grow and experience the development of their bodies. While in some families parents might respect the privacy of their children, especially when they are bathing, this wasn't the case in our house. Nearly every time Carter took a bath, Mumma told Carter she needed to get something out of her bedroom—which meant passing through the bathroom and seeing my sixteen year old brother lying fully exposed in the bathtub. At first, it seemed little more than an inconvenience. Carter, and then eventually Jack and I, would simply have to cover our genitals when Mumma came walking in. But as time passed, the walk-throughs occurred unannounced. And finally, she told us to leave the bathroom door open for the entire duration of our bath. She wanted to see us at all times—clothed or not—and it soon happened that my mother wanted us to see her as well.

Jack had spent the morning at Mr. Cosby's—an old neighbor of ours who every now and again paid us to help him deliver milk in the very early morning hours. As I lay in bed, I knew it was early without even opening my eyes because the sunlight always came in at that angle at that time of the morning. When I finally did open my eyes, I thought I would be alone, but I was not. Why Mumma was in my room at seven-thirty on a Saturday morning, I never would know. But there she was standing at the foot of my bed—her breasts bared, naked from the waist up. I squeezed my eyes shut and slid the sheet over my head, pretending that I was only moving in my sleep. As nausea crept up my throat, thoughts raced through my mind. I didn't know why she was there, or what she was doing. I only knew that something was terribly wrong. I lay still as long as I could, wondering if I should hold my breath and pretend I was dead.

Finally, after a few moments, I heard her walk away. I never asked her why she was there. And I never spoke about it at all.

After we moved from the farm, my mother's behavior grew even more erratic—especially for a woman who had drilled the catechism into me. The memories of Monday night trips to church to attend benediction made little sense to me anymore.

"Go on and tell Father you'll serve," she would demand while the priest was still in the sacristy.

"I don't wanna, Mumma," I would protest. "I did it last week."

"You are turning your back on Gawd," she would respond. "Ya know that."

Reluctantly, I would finally offer my services as an altar boy, convinced that if I didn't, I was denying all that was holy by not offering to assist the priest— even if it were just for one night.

After moving to the small neighborhood at the intersection of the few tarred roads, our new house became a place where my mother would eventually bring home men of nearly every age and color. She invited friends from her work—women who had husbands and children waiting at home—to come to our house. At our house, adultery was not only facilitated, but encouraged. Women would be joined by their lovers, to swoon on the back porch or to make use of my mother's room—to laugh and pretend that all was well with the world.

Just as my father had hidden stolen copper in the ground beneath our farmhouse a few years before,

Mumma was also now willing to use our new home not only as a hiding place for clandestine affairs, but for stolen goods as well. With only two medium-sized bedrooms and a tiny bathroom, our new house was small. Oddly enough, though, the garage attached to the house was large enough to hold two cars. Unfortunately, there was never any room for a car. A friend of hers, Mumma would explain, was in the trucking business and needed a place to store some of his merchandise. Her friend told her our garage would not only be the perfect size, but an ideal location as well. As it turned out, Mumma's friend was in the business of hi-jacking trucks. Our garage became the place for allowing hot items—usually liquor—ample time to cool off.

My mother also had her lovers. Perhaps she hoped that one of them would save her. Perhaps she was just lonely. There were men named Joe and Phil, Richard and Ray and others whose names I cannot remember. But of all those who came to our house, Floyd was the one who broke her heart.

Every Tuesday and Friday evening, just as the sun began to set, Floyd would arrive—he would drive his car around to the back of house, park it under the trees and then quietly step on to the back porch. With his hair slicked back and his face clean shaven, he tried his best to look the part of a dandy. The grease-stained hands, though, were enough to prove that he was a man whose job it was to change tires and pump gas every day except Sunday. Like all of the others,

Floyd was married with a family that lived not far from us, but he, Mumma said, was different.

Once a week, Floyd would give my mother a hundred dollars for whatever she needed. They never went out anywhere, never to a restaurant, never to a movie, never any place where they could be seen together.

"His wife is always lookin' for him," Mumma would explain. "Besides, I love him. I don't care where we are."

For more than a year, Floyd and my mother would sit in the living room of our house watching "Sanford and Son" on Friday nights, or if he couldn't make it on Friday, he would surely be there Saturday night to watch "Hee-Haw." The following fall, Floyd told my mother he had decided to leave his wife. Mumma was ecstatic. Finally, my mother thought, she would once again have a man of her own, but her dream was short-lived. Floyd's wife had found out about the affair and had threatened to "take every last dime." Floyd liked my mother, but not that much.

It was around four o'clock in the afternoon when Floyd called our house. As usual when he called, Mumma would stretch the cord from the phone on the wall in the kitchen, out the back door, and on to the porch. There she would sit—whispering and laughing. But not this time. Floyd told her that things were over between them; he wouldn't be coming over anymore. There would be no more visits, no phone calls—not even passing conversation. This was the end. By ten o'clock that same night, Mumma had decided that it was to be the end of her as well. She downed half a dozen valium.

Whenever my mother overdosed on pills, it was an unfortunate thing for my brothers and me. Not because she was depressed or took too many pills—but because she never took enough. In reality, my mother never really intended to kill herself—she only made it look that way. If she had intended to commit suicide, she would have taken the whole bottle—not just four or five. The fact that there were nearly twenty more pills left to take told me she just wanted someone to care about her. That was something each of us wanted for ourselves as well.

Just as in other times, my mother announced that she had taken an overdose of pills and that we should call Uncle Junie—who now lived only about ten minutes away.

"Tell 'im I tried to kill myself," she said. We did, and our uncle came. For a few minutes, he spoke to our mother—and then he left. Uncle Junie instructed us to keep her awake as long as we could, and so for the next few hours, my brothers and I walked our "helpless" mother up and down the short hallway, pouring black coffee into her. Eventually, though, Mumma went to sleep. The next morning, Uncle Junie took her to Richmond Memorial Hospital. There she was placed in the hospital's psychiatric ward which was more like a lock-down unit in the county jail more than anything else. She was given pills to sedate her—to keep her from making another attempt to kill herself—and taught to make ceramic ashtrays. She stayed there for two weeks.

For whatever reason—whether it was because of where we lived, where we had come from or what we had become—suicide was never really an uncommon occurrence in our world. It wasn't until long after I had finished college that I began to realize that most of my friends and college roommates had never known anyone at all who had died by their own hand. Sure, they had heard about a friend of a friend's third cousin who had taken their own life, but they hadn't actually known the person first-hand. It wasn't that way with us.

My aunt's mother had hung herself when I was very young. A man down the road from us on Roosevelt Avenue had shot himself. A kid in my tenth grade math class, Allen, had gone home after school to find his mother dead—sitting in the car in the garage with a vacuum cleaner hose taped to the exhaust pipe and into one of the car's back windows. There was a girl in my history class, Theresa, who shot herself in the head. Her aim was off a little bit, so instead of killing herself instantly, she spent a year in a nursing home in a vegetative-state. Then she died. The most painful memory, though, was from 1972. I was a junior in high school. He was a friend, someone I hung around with, a member of my Boy Scout troop—kid who sometimes just wanted to talk.

Jeff Carpenter was a year younger than me. He was soft-spoken, with a drawl a bit heavier than most. His hair was dark brown and fell over his forehead and ears as if someone had put a bowl on his head and cut around it. His skin had a little darker tone to it than most of the boys I knew and, except for a small birthmark on his left cheek, he had no blemishes at all—not even an occasional pimple. There might have been some Cherokee or Pamunkey blood in him. Our scoutmaster had asked him about it once, but in keeping with his shy demeanor—Jeff was embarrassed by the question. He said he didn't really know.

Like so many of the boys I knew—myself included—Jeff was desperate for a man in his life. His father had died when he was about five and his mumma was a lot older than most of our mothers. I had gotten a job after school working as a soda-jerk at Mechanicsville's drug store and Jeff pumped gas at the Esso across the street. The gas station closed at five, so whenever he finished work, my friend would stop in the drugstore for a Coca-Cola and pack of Nabs before heading home.

"Hey, Randy," Jeff said.

"Whadya doing tonight?" I asked him as he sat at the counter.

"Dunno," Jeff answered. "Got homework to do. I dunno." His eyes were sadder than usual that day, almost as if he were wondering if it was time to cry or not. We exchanged some small talk—wondering about the next time we could go dove hunting together. We spoke about school, about girls and about Mrs. Perkins, the teacher we hated most.

"Well," my friend said after finishing his snack. "I'll see ya."

"Okay," I answered. "See ya tomorrow."

Jeff left the drugstore that afternoon and went home. The next day, after his mother had left for work, Jeff didn't come to school. Instead, he got a can of gasoline from the shed and poured the contents throughout the house, leaving a trail up to the second floor. Then he lit a fire in the living room, climbed the stairs to his bedroom and locked himself in his room. Finally, with the same shotgun he had used on our autumn hunting trips, he sat on the edge of his bed and shot himself in the head. Jeff Carpenter was fifteen.

When my mother returned home after two weeks in the hospital, nothing much had changed. Other than us having a few more ashtrays in the house, things were pretty much the same—except Floyd didn't come over anymore. Instead, Mumma had new men. About every other month or so, men would come into her life, into our house and into my mother's bedroom—which was across the hall from mine. There, they would spend hours together—with my mother occasionally coming out for more cold beer. The house was old; the walls were thin; the doors were cheap. The sounds that filled our house those nights and evenings left their indelible mark. In the years that followed, Mumma returned to one psychiatric hospital after another. Sometimes she came out somewhat better, other times not so much.

Her last admission was during the fall of my freshman year of college (another slight overdose of pills, another call to a relative, and another stay in the mad house). By then, my brothers had moved out of the house. Carter had moved into an apartment of his own and had begun a work career and Jack was still in the Navy. Even though Vietnam was still a hotbed of action and the weekly casualty reports were still being announced on the evening news, Mumma had told him he had to go. So—without my father's knowledge—she signed him up for four years of active duty. He was only seventeen years old.

Now, it was just Mumma and me.

"You'll hafta quit school 'n take care of me," she told me the day I picked her up from the hospital.

"But I just started," I answered. "I've already taken out loans for school . . . ."

"I don't care," she said. "I'm not well enough to take care of myself. You'll have to take care of me."

The following day, I dropped my classes and found a job as a security guard on the college campus. At least I would be near a school, I told myself. After Christmas, I told my mother I had been accepted at a seminary in Philadelphia. I would be leaving Mechanicsville, so she would have to find someone else to take care of her. Mumma went back to work that January.

A few years later, my mother would find another abusive alcoholic to marry again, as strange as it seemed, another man named Jackson. After that, she would try again—another marriage and more attempts at suicide. She failed at each of them and her life would continue its vicious cycle. Throughout her life, it always seemed as if my mother was always trying to find the man she wanted but never had in either a father or a husband. And after my father had left, when she could not find them in the men she slept with—in some twisted fashion, she tried to find that elusive lover in her sons. I wonder if that is why—unlike Jolene—Mumma never left Daddy. She never packed her bags and her children in the car to drive off while Daddy was at work. Mumma wasn't strong enough to do that. She couldn't bring herself to admit that she was addicted to men like my father. Men who would use her and tempt her with the thought of something she never had.

Part Twelve

After a few more minutes of revisiting other faces in the parlor, I made my way over to the priest.

"Hello, Father," I said shaking the priest's hand, "I'm one of Jackson's sons."

"I'm very sorry for your loss," he responded. "I'm Father Jenkins."

"Are you leading the funeral service tomorrow?" I asked.

"Yes, I am," he said.

Thoughts quickly began to whirl through my mind. *What could this man possibly say about my father to the people who stood in this room, people who still bore the wounds of his transgressions?* What could he ever say to me, to Carter, Jack, Thomas—and the list went on.

"Do you know much about my father?" I asked.

"Well, for the last few months your father and I met every Monday," the priest continued. "He wasn't well enough to come to Mass, so I would bring him Holy Communion and then we would pray together. He liked to pray the rosary. We talked quite a bit—at least your brother tells me it was a lot for your father," he laughed.

"Do you know much about his past?" I asked. I was determined to drive to the core of my intent.

"Well, no," Father Jenkins continued. "That's something he never talked much about. We mostly talked about what was going on in his life now, what his concerns were. Your father knew he was a very sick man . . . that his health was deteriorating rapidly."

"I wanna tell you about my father," I said. I wondered for a moment. Could Daddy have told him about what he did? Everything? Did he hold *anything* back? Did he talk about that time in the farmhouse— in my bedroom? No, this priest wasn't going to tell me anything. I knew the rules; he couldn't say anything. But that didn't mean I couldn't tell him. *Sorry for my loss? You have no idea.* But before I could say anything more, Carter called to me from across the room, trying to get my attention. "Excuse me, Father, I'll come back."

Moving across the room, I eased past slightly familiar faces—all the while glancing toward my brother to see who it was he was talking to—who it was he had wanted me to see. I really wasn't anxious to become reacquainted with another relative whom I'd forgotten long ago, or one who would tell me how much weight I had put on in the past thirty years. Nor did I want to try to remember the name of someone who knew me from one of the old neighborhoods, or who knew my parents "way back win."

When I reached Carter, the woman standing next to him turned toward me. Now, in full view, I gazed upon the face of someone I had truly longed to see again—and the years had been kind to her.

"You know who this is?" Carter asked with an approving smile.

"Annie," I said ignoring my brother. "My God, it's good to see you. What a wonderful surprise . . . ."

"I hope it's okay I'm here," she started. "I never really met your father, but I saw the obituary in the paper and figured you would be in town so . . . ."

"Yes, yes," I interrupted, "This is terrific. I'm so glad you came."

Of all the people I would have wanted to see at that moment, or any other moment for that matter, it was Annie. We hadn't seen each other nor spoken in more than thirty years, but—had we encountered each other in some other setting—I still would have recognized her. Her deep brown eyes and broad smile were framed in the same chestnut hair that attracted me to her when I was ten years old.

In 1966, I was the new kid in Mrs. Culler's fifth grade class at the Mechanicsville Elementary School. Before then, the only school I had attended was a Catholic school in Richmond, so to be in a public school—amidst publicans—made for a most terrifying few weeks. During my first days, there were only one or two kids who had offered me any kind of welcome. One of them was Annie.

Every person can recall their first true love. It's one of life's universal experiences. But for me to say that Annie was my first love would be an understatement. She was the first human being whose presence touched the depth of my soul. Seeing her each day made me forget—if even for just a few hours—the madness and savagery that were so much a part of daily life. Perhaps it was for this that I loved her most of all.

During those first weeks of school, I stuttered and stammered whenever I tried to speak to her. Simple phrases and greetings turned into exasperating calisthenics for my mouth and tongue. Expressing anything more than a one syllable word or grunt meant risking humiliation at my lack of oral coordination. But it didn't seem to matter to her and—despite my repeated embarrassment—whatever conversations we had were the highlight of my day.

Even though we saw each other every school day for more than eight years, ours was not a constant relationship. But there were two occasions when we became so close that my heart ached from the awe of love.

The first time was on a December day when we were in the sixth grade. As was often the practice back then, the girls left for the lunch room a good five or ten minutes before the boys. The head start gave them time to go to the lavatory and do whatever it was that girls had to do in the bathroom before heading to the cafeteria. One particular morning as the girls prepared to leave the classroom, Annie passed by my desk. Being that the aisles created between the rows of our school desks were narrow, my heart began to race at the thought that the dress that fell just below her knees might brush my clothing. I became even more excited as I imagined catching a glimpse of the face of the girl who could provide such comfort to my spirit with her smile—instead of seeing just the back of her head as was so often the case since she sat in the front of the room. Within a moment, as she appeared full-view, I felt a warmth in my face as my hands began to sweat. Finally, Annie's eyes were looking at mine. Without a word, she walked toward me—closer than I ever could have imagined. As she approached, her hand reached out for mine. Quickly she passed a small piece of paper to me and as she did our fingers brushed against one another. For an ever-so-brief moment, I felt her warmth. Working carefully to avoid being noticed by our teacher, I stuffed the note into my pocket and waited until lunch time when I would be able to read her message. In the few minutes that followed, I spent hours imagining what message might be written on the piece of paper that rested in my pocket. Could it be that she was feeling for me the same depth of love and adulation I had for her? Finally, after the girls had left the room and the boys were called to file out for lunch, I headed to a table far off in the corner of the cafeteria which would provide me the sense of privacy I longed for.

Opening its lid, I stood my lunchbox on its side to make a small barrier that would protect my actions from the eyes of anyone who might be watching. I unfolded the paper and silently read her message.

I like you. Do you like me? had been penciled carefully on a fragment torn from a composition book. Beneath the questions were two small boxes where I was supposed to check off my response: one beside the word "yes," another next to the word "no." I quickly made a large X in the yes box and re-folded the note. After lunch, as our class gathered at the lunch room doors to line up for our walk back to the room, I passed the message back to her. This time, though, our hands did not touch; we only smiled. But that was enough.

Through the days and weeks that followed, Annie and I often spoke on the playground. In February, we exchanged Valentines which somehow made our relationship official. That winter, I carved our initials deep into the side of a very large beech tree in the woods behind that old farmhouse where my brothers and I had been terrorized by our father. An outline of a heart surrounded our initials and two long lines created an arrow piercing the heart. Beneath the image, I carved the year; it was 1968.

During the next few years, as we moved through junior high school, we found reasons to talk on the telephone. We called each other with questions about homework or to talk about something special which might have happened during the day. But deeper in our teen years, all that seemed to change. As my life and that of my brothers became more violent and disconnected, the regular phone conversations ended. Weeks turned into months and the months turned into years. Eventually, we simply became teenagers who attended the same school. After all, my family had pretty much fallen apart and I didn't want anyone getting close enough to see the carnage.

If my father had ever fought to stay sober, by the time I had reached my teen years, the battle was over. Daddy had completely surrendered. The regular verbal tirades, smackings, and belt-whippings he had launched against us when were we younger now gave way to "battles of wit" as he called them—moments of mental torture and emotional abuse. The decay that had long ago claimed his body had now begun to take hold of his mind as well.

By April of our senior year, Annie and I seemed to be moving closer to each other once again. Even though we weren't in any of the same classes, we had begun spending time together a few days a week . . . talking during lunch, or during a Friday night football game or a basketball game. And just as we had in years before, we managed to find a reason to call each other on the telephone. There never really was anything so pressing it couldn't have waited until the next school day—but those conversations gave us an opportunity to reminisce about the times we had shared since we'd first met in the fifth grade. We spoke of the teachers and classmates we had known, about songs and dances and the things that made us laugh. Every now and again one of us would mention how special our friendship was and how it would undoubtedly change once we had graduated. And then, finally, during one of those phone calls that seemed to be resurrecting a sweet depth to our friendship, it happened.

"How do you like the theme of the prom?" Annie asked after a slight pause in our conversation.

"Uh, I like it a lot," I answered.

"Yeah," she continued, "it's from the Three Dog Night song, 'Pieces of April,'"

"Uh huh."

"Are ya going?" she asked.

"Where?"

"To the prom."

"I'm not sure," I answered.

"I wanna go," she said, "but nobody's asked me yet." And with that, there was silence.

In my head, I heard a dozen voices yelling at me—echoing—telling me what to do and what not to do, what to say and how to say it, how to speak without seeming too excited while making sure I didn't come across as too eager or anxious. As I allowed myself to imagine the joy of taking Annie to the prom, I wondered if it could really happen. Where would I get the money for a suit, or for flowers, or dinner?

"Oh," I mumbled, unsure of what I could or should say. "I don't know what I'm gonna do. I'll probably make my mind up in a day or so."

"Oh," she responded.

Once our conversation ended, I sat and looked at the telephone, still somewhat lost in the wonder of the occasion. As my thoughts began to unfold, I found a piece of paper and pencil and began to estimate and calculate how much money I would need in order to make the prom a reality for Annie and me. The cost of renting a suit was more than I could earn in two weeks—and the prom was exactly ten days away. Then there would be the dinner and flowers. I would also need money for gas. But what would I do for a car? As my mother came in to the kitchen, she saw me writing numbers, only to scratch through them and write new ones—all in an attempt to make them add up to something I could afford.

"What are you working on?" she asked.

"I wanna go to the prom," I said, still staring at the numbers on the paper. "There's this girl I know and I wanna take her and . . . I really wanna go." I didn't go on any further in my explanation.

"You are gonna need about seventy-five or a hundred dollars," my mother shot back. "When you figure the suit, flowers, all that. Can't do it for anything less." There was a brief silence as she turned from me and headed back to the living room.

"If you really wanna go," she continued as she left the kitchen, "you are gonna have to ask your Daddy for money. Good luck with that."

Mumma made no secret of the fact that my father had not given her any money since he'd moved out more than a few years before. Once our electricity and water had begun to be shut off on a regular basis—

because we couldn't pay the bills—my Uncle Carlton gave my mother a job answering the phone at his repair shop. It didn't pay much, but it kept the lights on in our house. To Mumma, Jesus was more likely to return on a cloud of glory before my father was going to give me any money for the prom. And maybe if it had been some other girl, I might not have given the idea any more thought. But this was Annie.

Even though the next day was Saturday, my mother still had to work—which meant it would be early evening before I could make the drive to Daddy's. It also meant I would be running the risk of getting to my father's after he spent most of the day drinking. But it was a risk I had to take.

When Mumma got home, I headed to my father's. Daddy didn't have a phone—he said it kept people from bothering him—but since the only time he left his trailer was to either go to work or to get beer, it was a pretty good bet he would be home when I got there. Alcohol had consumed my father just as much as he had consumed it—and it was apparent in the way he and his second family now lived: without much furniture, in an old rusted-out trailer that sat tucked away in some far-off corner of what the sign out front called a "mobile home park." His favorite family member was a mangy dog he kept on a chain. The dog's constant dragging of the chain—back and forth from one end of the trailer to the other—had long ago worn away any grass that might have once been there. As a result, the April rains had left the ground a muddy mixture of red clay and dog crap.

As I pulled up to Daddy's trailer, the dog began barking and yelping, announcing my arrival. My father stood in the doorway, looking to see who had come a' callin'.

"Shut up, Heinz," he yelled to the dog. I stepped carefully through the muddy mix and up the wooden steps, wiping my feet hard before going in.

"Hey boy, whadya up to? Come on in here," my father said.

"Hey, Daddy," I said giving him a hug and a kiss on the cheek. "How ya been?"

"I'm awright," he answered. "You wanna Pepsi-Cola?"

"No, thanks, I'm okay. Where is everybody?"

"Jolene and the kids are up in Spotsylvania. They'll be back tonight."

I sat down on the couch across from my father. He looked at me and then back to the television in the corner. The rabbit ears on top of the set were wrapped in aluminum foil. It helped make the reception a bit less snowy, but not much.

"Goddamn piece a shit," my father said. "Never can get much of a picture. Go over there and move those rabbit ears to the right." I walked over to the set and slid the antennas slowly to the side. The blurry images on the television screen still seemed to be making their way through a snow storm.

"Never mind," he mumbled. "Goddamn piece a shit anyway."

As I sat back down, I argued with myself, wondering if I should tell him about the prom now, or should I wait until we had more time warming up to one another. Waiting for another hour or so would risk waiting until he was drunker and more irritated, which would make him more likely to argue about anything I would say. On the other hand, I reasoned, if I spoke too soon, I risked seeming like nothing more than a person who was after his money. The fact of the matter, though, was that my father had not offered any financial support to his family in more than a few years—and so, I deduced, perhaps he would realize this, ask for forgiveness, and help me out in any way he could. That became my plan. Just a few more minutes of small talk and I would do it.

"Daddy?" I said looking down at the floor just in front of him.

"Yeah?"

"I need a favor."

"Yeah? Whadya need?" he answered in a low, somber voice.

"Well, the prom is coming up in a couple weeks and there's this girl I really wanna take . . . ."

"Yeah?"

"Well, I need to borrow about seventy-five dollars for everything—the suit, flowers . . . ."

My father sat silently for a moment, his eyes staring through me. "Goddamn you," Daddy began. "You son of a bitch. You bring your ass in here and think you can just come here when you want and say 'Daddy, gimme some money.' Your Mumma sent you here, didn't she, boy? Flowers! I'll get some flowers 'n shove 'em down your goddamn throat . . . your mother . . . ." What else my father shouted after that, I couldn't say. Once his tone had begun to take on that of a mad dog, I no longer heard what foamed from his mouth. As his sounds grew into screams, I wondered how long it would be before he began swinging fists or reaching for one of the knives lying on the counter nearby. Hurrying out of the trailer through the mud and dog crap and into the car, I could still hear the sounds of his curses as his voice blended with the barking of his dog. Our visit was over.

The following Monday I returned to school and, for weeks thereafter, I avoided Annie. We didn't see each other at lunch, or in the gym, or in the hallways between classes. If I didn't see her, I thought, then perhaps these imaginings of the prom, of spending time together, of experiencing such a splendid moment of grace—would eventually fade from my life. There were no telephone calls or friendly conversations between us . . . not even a smile. As the ten days slowly passed, when that Friday night finally arrived, I found myself sitting alone in my room. Later that summer, Annie started college. I, for my part, moved on, too—far away from the people who were my family.

In the years that followed, whenever I thought about those whom I had known in Richmond so long ago, I would often wonder where Annie was or what she might be doing at that particular moment. Now, as we stood in the funeral parlor reminiscing about days long past and catching up on each other's lives, I could not help but wonder how different my life might have been had I spent just a few hours with someone who brought so much hope to one young boy.

Part Thirteen

For the next hour or so, I spoke to men and women, old friends and acquaintances, hearts I had not encountered for decades. I was beckoned from one corner of the parlor to another. Some of the conversations lasted far too long, others not long enough. Among those who called out to me, though, there was one of which I was particularly delighted to hear. Even today, the recollection of its raspy melody brings nothing but delight. It belonged to an old neighbor, Mr. Kersley.

Ashby and Barbara Kersley had lived in the house next door to us when I was born. They had children roughly the same age as my brothers and me, and once a week "Uncle Ash" and "Aunt Bobbi"—as they came to be known—even played pinnacle with Mumma and Daddy. They weren't really any relation to my family, but at some point in time—far too early for me to remember—Ashby and Barbara and my parents decided we were too close, too familiar, for us to continue addressing them as Mr. and Mrs. Kersley. So a more familiar title was adopted. Like all good Southern children, we were expected to continue using the appropriate salutations of "sir" and "ma'am" when addressing them, but we could dispense with the formal stuff.

Uncle Ash was a bear of a man. He stood more than six feet tall and weighed at least two hundred and thirty pounds. He was a working man, with large tattooed arms that reminded me of Popeye. His voice was raspy, almost hoarse. I never knew if it was from polyps on his vocal cords or from yelling at his children, or both. Whatever the case, he was a fearsome fellow. Despite his girth, though, Ashby Kersley was kind-hearted, loving, outwardly affectionate to his wife, and protective of his daughters. He was a good man.

After their youngest child, Karen, was born, the Kersleys moved out of the house next door into a three bedroom, brick rancher they built about ten minutes away. Of course we didn't see them as often as we had, but the times when we did see them were fun and memorable. My earliest memory of visiting their new house was during an overnight stay when I was five years old. A few weeks before, I had broken my leg while jumping from the top of a fence in my backyard, so I had a cast which extended from my hip all the way down to the tips of my toes. Their son, Timmy, and I were the best of friends. Whenever we were together, we usually blew up toy soldiers with firecrackers or worked at building a fort. But since my leg was in a cast, the only thing we could do was lie on the floor in his living room and play with his matchbox cars.

"It's time for bed, boys," Aunt Bobbi said as the evening wore on. "Timmy, you sleep in your bed and Randy you're gonna sleep in Dougie's bed." Dougie was the oldest son who was spending the night at a friend's house that night. "Timmy, you go brush your teeth," she continued. "Randy, you hold on a minute and I'm gonna carry you into the other room."

Aunt Bobbi scooped me up and carried me into the bathroom. After I brushed my teeth, she carried me into the bedroom and laid me in Dougie's bed. "Sleep tight," she said, and kissed me on the forehead.

The next morning as the sun began to warm the bedroom, I woke up to the strangest situation. At some point during the night, I had slid to the far side of the bed and my leg was now wedged deep within the space between the wall. My face was pressing against the wallpaper. I couldn't move. I was upside down and sideways all at the same time. "Bobbi," I yelled—forgetting to add the title. I had heard Uncle Ashby yell the same thing so many times and it always seemed to evoke an immediate response. "Bobbi," I screamed again.

A second later, she came running into the bedroom. "What's wrong?"

"I'm stuck."

In the years that followed, both she and Uncle Ashby retold that story over and over again to anyone who would listen. Laughing just as hard with each telling as they had the day it happened. I laughed, too.

Unlike many of the people who flowed in and out of my life throughout the years, the Kersleys remained constant. Even though great spans of time would eventually go by without any real communication between us, whenever we would reconnect, it always seemed that we easily fell back into the rhythm of familiarity that comes through deep friendship.

If the Kersleys knew about the troubles between Mumma and Daddy as well as the whippings my brothers and I received, they never said anything. But then again, there were times when Aunt Bobbi and Uncle Ash displayed overwhelming kindness towards Carter, Jack, and me. Whenever they invited one of us to a movie or an overnight stay, I would wonder if it was a coincidence that their invitation had come after one of my father's drunken rampages.

In the summer after I graduated from high school, Uncle Ash knew I needed work to support Mumma and me.

"Be at Berks Oil at 7:30 Monday morning," he said in his signature rasp.

"What am I gonna do?" I asked.

"You're gonna be delivering oil."

"You mean to houses?"

"Goddamn, boy," he said laughing, "what do you think I mean?"

"Whose gonna drive the truck?" I asked.

"You are."

"But I don' know how to drive a truck."

"You'll learn."

The following Monday, I made the short drive to Berks Oil Company. While it sounded impressive, Berks Oil Company was basically an old gas station Ned Berks had bought. He constructed a few large oil storage tanks out back and, when they weren't out delivering home heating oil, there were a couple of small tanker trucks parked in a field next to the tarmac. Over the weekend, I had purchased a pair of green coveralls just like the ones I had seen Ashby Kersley wear.

"James Randolph," It was his standard greeting to me. "You ready?"

"Yessir," I walked towards the passenger's door of the truck and began to climb in.

"Where you goin?" Uncle Ash said. "You 'a drivin'."

"But I don't know how to drive a truck."

"Well, nobody ever learned by watchin' somebody else drive. Get over there," he said pointing to the driver's door.

I walked around to the driver's side, reached for the door handle and pulled myself up into the cab. "What do I do first?"

"First thing you do is pray that you don't kill us both in this thing," he said laughing. I pushed in the clutch, turned the key and for the next six hours guided the truck down gravel roads, dirt lanes, and rural roads. By Wednesday, I had only backed over one mailbox, which Uncle Ashby figured wasn't too bad. On Friday afternoon, though, my progress was set back a bit when I turned into a driveway and pulled a little too close to a well that was located about six feet away from the gravel. Less than a minute after I shifted the gears into neutral, the weight of a truck filled with home heating oil caused the ground beneath the back tires to shift and a sink hole was forming quickly. The shifting dirt displaced the surrounding soil and within a moment the well I had only casually noticed a few minutes earlier had now caved in.

"Put it in gear and get us out of here," Ashby shouted. "This thing's gonna swallow the truck and us along with it."

Forgetting to press in the clutch, the gears began grinding and groaning.

"The clutch," Ashby hollered.

I pressed the pedal and slammed the shifter into first gear. The truck heaved and swayed from one side to the other, lurching forward with the back tires slowly rolling out of the giant sink hole.

"What about the oil?" I asked.

"What about it?"

"Are we still gonna fill her tank?"

"Not today," Ashby continued, "we're gettin' outta here. I'll talk to Mr. Berks. We'll figure somethin' out." We called it an afternoon.

The following week, Uncle Ashby continued to ride along with me, carefully giving me directions on what to avoid when pulling into driveways. I learned what situations to avoid including stretches of highway that included weigh stations.

"Stay off of 64," Ashby stated. "You can't go through a weigh station."

I couldn't understand his reasoning, especially since the interstate highway had just been finished and would easily cut time off of any deliveries in the surrounding counties.

"How come?" I asked.

"When Ned bought this truck, we did some modifications to the tanks so it would hold more oil. It's way overweight. That's why it sank so fast into that lady's well last week. If you pull into the weigh station, they'll shut this thing down."

The following Monday, I pulled into Berks Oil Company, got the truck keys and filled the large tanker with heating oil in preparation for the deliveries we would be making during the day. Uncle Ashby called me over toward the small room that served as the main office.

"I think you're ready to do this on your own," he said smiling. "Here's the deliveries for the day. Be careful." Handing me a small stack of billing tickets, he turned and walked back into the office.

"Are you sure?" I shouted after him.

"We'll find out," he laughed.

In the weeks that followed, I gradually mastered the skills required to get the truck into just the right position to deliver heating oil into tanks without causing any significant damage such as knocking over mailboxes or crushing flowerbeds. After more than a month without incident, I was comfortable in my ability and wondered what it would be like to do this for the rest of my life.

In 1974, Mechanicsville was still a sleepy little village in rural Virginia, but old farms were quickly being sold and turned into neighborhoods with paved roads and tri-level houses. One of those new developments was Cranybrook Meadows. In the near month that I had been delivering oil, I had made deliveries to farms and old houses hidden down dirt roads and gravel lanes. But this was my first time into one of the neighborhoods where—as my mother would say—the other half lived. The houses in Cranybrook Meadows were all built of red brick. Nearly all of them had wrought iron railings along their porches. Each house had white trim. I used to think that everybody in the neighborhood must be happy, since they had a nice house and pretty lawns. But a couple of kids I knew in high school lived here. One of them, Dennis, shot himself. Another kid, Allison, had found her mother inside the family car parked in the garage. The motor was still running. Not everyone in that neighborhood was happy.

As I turned the truck into the development, I remembered Uncle Ashby's caution to me about driving in neighborhoods. "Slow down," he would say. "People will call Mr. Berks and complain. And you'll be out of a job in a heartbeat." This morning, I made sure no one could say I was driving too fast.

The house where I was to make my delivery sat back off the street about fifty yards. It was a red brick tri-level with large maple trees in the front yard and a long asphalt driveway lined with azalea bushes. I imagined that in the spring, the bushes would be aglow with red, purple and white pastels. In all honesty, I was struck by the beauty of the place, even if the people might not be happy here.

I pulled the truck to the side of the road, stopping directly in front of the driveway. Ashby had told me that fuel oil will dissolve asphalt so I needed to make sure I didn't spill any whenever I was near a driveway. I took the truck out of gear and put it in neutral. Almost in the same motion, I pulled the switch which turned on the pump on the back of the truck. As I climbed out of the cab, I was still caught up in the beauty of the neighborhood. The well-manicured lawns, the coordinating trim of the houses, the pristine driveways. I glanced down at the delivery ticket in my hand. "Fill" was printed across the top. As I had done more than a hundred times by now, I pulled the long, thick hose from the truck and threw it over my shoulder. Tugging it down the driveway, I was careful not to let any oil drip out of the nozzle and onto the surface beneath my feet. Near the end of the driveway, in the flower bed next to the house, was my target—a large steel pipe jutting out of the ground. The pipe led to an underground tank that could hold 1,000 gallons of heating oil. A family could fill it up and not have to worry about being cold all winter long. Attached to the pipe, just above ground-level, was a second pipe. That was the whistle. Whenever someone filled the tank, the pipe would emit a soft whistling sound. When it stopped, I would know that the tank was full.

After pushing the nozzle firmly into the fill-pipe, I locked the handle so that the oil would keep flowing without my having to hold the handle for several minutes. After a second, the whistling began and I stood up, looked around, and took in the beauty of the morning. I looked at the houses, the trees surrounding them, the trimmed shrubbery. I gazed across the street, laughing a bit at how the whole neighborhood seemed to match. "Mumma would like this place," I said to myself. "She always wanted things in our house to match." As I continued to enjoy the scenery, I noticed the hose leading from the truck drawing tight. Within a second, it was so taut that the hose had now lifted off the ground. The sequence of things that followed only took an instant. The nozzle—with the handle still locked so as to allow the oil to flow freely—popped out of the fill pipe. At a rate of a few gallons per second, fuel oil flooded the asphalt, the azaleas, the lawn and everything else in its path. I was finally able to grab the nozzle and quickly click it off. I held tightly on to the hose as it pulled me down the driveway towards the truck.

"What's going on?" I shouted, though no one was around to hear or answer me.

Finally realizing that the truck was rolling down the street, I grabbed enough of the hose to hold with both hand. For a moment I thought I could keep the truck from rolling further down the street by pulling the hose toward me. It didn't work. I dropped the hose and ran as fast as I could, imagining that if I just pushed myself a little harder, I could catch up with the truck, grab on to the door, pull myself into the cab and stop the truck. I had a good imagination. As the truck continued to roll down the street, it quickly gained momentum, but I continued to run after it. Twenty yards, thirty, forty, fifty—it kept going. After traveling nearly the length of a football field, the large tires began to veer off to the right, onto the gravel shoulder, then over a mailbox, through one of the nicest flowerbeds I had ever seen. It finally came to a stop inside a large yew just ten feet from the brick steps which led to the front door of one of the houses. Exhausted from the tug-of-war, the chase, and the terror which held me, I stood at the edge of the lawn—not sure what to do.

After a moment, I walked up the front steps and rang the doorbell. An elderly woman pushed aside a white curtain next to the door and stared at me. Her mouth didn't move.

"My truck rolled into your front yard," I said in a loud voice. "Can I use your phone to call the office?"

The woman stared at me, still not speaking. My coveralls were covered with oil. My hands and arms were coated as well. Finally, she shook her head.

Are you kidding me? "Okay, then," I said. "Can you please call the number right here?" I pulled a ballpoint pen out of my top pocket. "It's printed right there . . . just underneath Berks Oil Company."

The old woman opened the door just enough for me to slip the pen to her. "Just ask for Leroy," I continued. "Tell him one of his trucks is in your front yard."

Leroy Cox, a short, thin man in his late fifties, managed the business whenever Ned Berks was out of town. And Mr. Berks had left the office that morning for a long weekend at his place in the mountains. As I stood in the front lawn waiting for Leroy, I found some things to be thankful for. I was thankful that I wasn't in the truck when it ran into the lady's front yard. I was thankful that I had been able to turn the flow of oil off before the hose reached the street. I was thankful that the truck had veered off the road before rolling into the intersection about fifty yards further down the lane. And I was thankful that Leroy Cox was coming instead of Ned Berks.

"Son," Leroy began before he could even get out of his pickup truck, "what did you do?"

"I forgot to put the hand brake on," I explained. I had deduced that while I was waiting for Leroy. "I started pumping the oil, which I guess shifted some of the weight around inside and, before I knew it, it was rolling down the street. I ran after it, hoping I could catch it. I was able to click off the nozzle, but a lot spilled on that guy's driveway and azaleas. I guess I'm lucky it stopped here."

Leroy stood there shaking his head. He didn't seem very interested in my theories of why the truck had rolled down the street—only that it had. He walked slowly around the tanker, still sitting in the front yard of the lady's house—making his way from one side to the other.

"Tell you what," he said. "You take the pickup and go on back to the office. You can be done for today. I'll call a wrecker and get this thing pulled out of here. Be careful."

"She wouldn't let me use the phone," I said walking away. "She probably won't let you in either."

"She'll let me in," Leroy answered. "She's my aunt."

The following Monday, I showed up at work. Just as with any other morning, I met Ashby in the office. Leroy Cox was there, too. They were both laughing when I walked in.

"James Randolph," Uncle Ashby said, handing me the keys.

"Be careful," Leroy said. "Thank God Ned's not here."

I later found out that Uncle Ashby had convinced Leroy that the hand brake could have malfunctioned. That it was somehow possible that I had put the handbrake on, but that the shifting of the oil inside the tank could have allowed the brake to slip. I knew better.

Part Fourteen

At eight o'clock sharp, Father Jenkins quietly called everyone's attention and explained how my father had requested that a rosary be prayed during his wake. Since so many of the visitors were non-Catholics, the priest gave a brief explanation of the prayers and the significance of each oration. He then launched into a rapid recitation of the Rosary and what might usually have taken a prayerful person twenty minutes or so to ponder had been completed in seven minutes. I figured that the priest was either uncomfortable with leading such a personal, Catholic devotion among so many who were not of the faith, or that he had some place to be by eight-thirty. But since he was out of the parlor and leaving the funeral home as soon as the last Amen was said, it must have been that he had some place to be. *Tomorrow*, I thought. *I'll speak with him first thing.*

Once the room was nearly empty, I made my way toward the casket. At first, I considered not getting too close. I had always been afraid of my father in life, never quite sure what was going to come from his lips. Even into his eighties, whenever I was in his presence, my gut gnarled and trembled. Now as he lay dead in his casket, ten feet away, I figured I was at a safe distance. I was close enough that I could see what remained of him.

"He isn't gonna bite you—he's dead," Jack said coming up quietly behind me. "You can get closer." My brothers and I were the only ones left in the parlor.

It didn't look like Daddy. Corpses never do look like their owners. Those who attempt to console with phrases such as, "he looks like he's sleeping," or even worse, "isn't he so handsome," always seem to be either blind or filling the air with prattle as they struggle in their loss for words, for such words bring neither comfort nor consolation.

I'm still scared of him. I'll always be scared of him.

"He's gone," Carter said. "Let him go."

"You know," I continued, "even though he was eighty-two years old and a hundred and ten pounds— hell, I had to lift him into bed last time I saw him—I was always afraid of him. I don't think I'll ever stop being afraid of him. Is that just me?"

"When I was stationed in Norfolk," Jack began, "right after I got back from Vietnam, I got a pass to come home. I don't remember exactly how long it was for. Maybe a week or so. I decided not to tell Mumma or Daddy. I wanted to surprise them. I hitched a ride from Norfolk and got to Daddy's trailer sometime about 8:00 that night. You know what it was like. That goddamn dog barking his head off. The place smelled like dog shit. When I got there, the kids were in bed. Daddy was drunk. Of course, he was surprised to see me. Asked me how I was doing. What I had been up to, and I'm thinking, 'well, I just got back from fucking Vietnam, so really not much.'

"Not long after that, he kept talking about this and that and then—out of some fucking place in his crazy mind—he accused me of having sex with Jolene. So I thought, 'oh shit—here we go.'

"Well," Jack continued, "to Daddy, I was still a fourteen year old boy he could smack around. But the reality was I was nineteen years old, had gone through basic training, and had been in more than enough bar fights. I could take care of myself.

"So he came up out of that chair swinging his fists. I went at him just as hard and slammed him against the wall. I pinned his arms down by his sides. He kept trying to get loose. Spitting and cussing me. Calling me this and that. Jolene just stood there looking at us. Finally, he calmed down and I left.

"A couple days later, I went back. He was angry 'cause he had bruises all over his sides and arms from where I'd pinned him down. I'd squeezed him hard."

Jack laughed. "That's when I told him, 'Look, we can get along and act like a father and son or I can walk out that door and you'll never see me again. Ever. But you know what? You're never gonna hit me again.' That's when I stopped being afraid of him."

"Uh," Carter grunted. "Randy, just let it go. We all went through shit with him. Just let it go."

I stood there for a moment. I looked at the casket. I couldn't decide if I wanted to tell them what had happened in the bedroom of the farmhouse. I wasn't sure how I would even start the conversation. Daddy had done a lot of things to us. Whippings, beatings, curses, damnation. But to have sex with one of his sons?

Just let it go. I had tried that all my life. But some things just can't be let go. Did he ever try to have sex with you guys? I couldn't have been more graphic in my description without vomiting. In reality, though, I said nothing. The three of us just stared at my father.

The farmhouse that used to be on Shady Grove Road is still there. I've driven by the old place for more than forty years now. Can't really help it. The old clapboard house that used to sit far off the road amid acres of soybean fields now rests just off I-295 that skirts Richmond. As I make my way east onto the by-pass, I know it's coming. I save up my spit—a mouthful of snot and saliva—rolling down the window while slowing the car down enough to spew my fluids in the direction of the house. I curse it. Using every curse or vulgar word I can think of to let anyone with earshot know what had happened there. I am always alone in the car, though. No one really hears me. No one ever hears me. It has always been something I have never been able to speak of.

I don't remember if I had had my birthday yet. Maybe it was *on* my birthday. That would have made sense. Daddy giving me something to remember him by on my birthday. I do remember that it happened in the summer. A large cloud of dust had announced Daddy's visit, the big green Pontiac bouncing through the potholes that marked the long dirt road leading to the house. Mumma and I were the only ones at the house. I do remember that. When Daddy arrived, I was in the kitchen talking to Mumma. Even though I don't exactly remember all the details of his arrival, I suppose he came through the kitchen door. He always did. It was the only door anyone ever used to come and go. After saying hello and giving him the obligatory kiss on the cheek, I would have gone either upstairs or outside. That day, I went upstairs.

Through the vent in the upstairs floor, I could hear my parents talking about mundane things. Dogs. The corn growing on the acre down the hill. Rats in the basement. Mumma would have been hoping Daddy was going to give her some money before he left. Even if it was just twenty dollars or so. Mumma asked Daddy if he was hungry. He laughed and said yes.

"You want me to fix you something to eat?" Mumma said. Daddy was already on his way upstairs.

"Yeah." Daddy liked bologna sandwiches with mayonnaise.

No matter how hard I try, there are a lot of things I cannot recall about that day. It's strange, I suppose. I do remember other things, though. Some with great detail. The bedroom Jack and I shared. The color of the walls. The sheets on the bed. The floor. I remember the torn shades on the windows. The sheer curtains that had once been white.

It was a big bedroom, just at the top of the long staircase that wound its way through the center of the house. While there were only two single beds in our room, we could easily have put in two more and still had space left over. There were a couple of closets. The walls were made of plaster-covered lattice work which was common for houses built in the 1820s. At some point—long before we had moved in—someone had put up wallpaper, a floral print of tiny rose buds. The floor was made of wide wooden planks which had been painted nearly the same shade of duck-shit yellow as our old kitchen had been. The doors were white, with more than a dozen coats of paint layered on, the knobs white porcelain. All of the woodwork was white.

I was sitting on the floor when Daddy started coming up the steps. The stairs leading up the center of the house were bare wood, without carpet or covering—so with each step, his clumsy steps echoed off the walls giving a heightened sense of doom. The old man never came upstairs. Never. As soon as he started the long climb upstairs, I should have known he was up to something. All these years later, I've recalled the moment I heard his foot hit the final step at the top of the stairs just outside of my bedroom door. It was a strange experience, if nothing else. A sound I had never heard before. My father's foot coming to rest just outside of my bedroom door. In one regard, there was a sense of dread, perhaps fear. Nausea, maybe.

Daddy was smiling when he came in my room.

"Wha' you doin?" he asked. It was a standard phrase my father would utter in a mushy drawl. Even to the day he died, he would still say it the same way.

"Nothin. Just reading."

"Sit on the bed," he said stepping into the room. I did as he told me. He was quiet for a moment. He stood staring at me.

"I've got a secret to tell you," he began. "Now," he continued—looking at me and smiling, "you can't tell ya Mumma, or ya brothers or anybody." He was still smiling. "Ok?" His breathing was heavy. I wondered if he was out of breath from climbing the stairs. He stared at me, watching my face— occasionally glancing at my neck and chest.

"Ok," I answered. I remember thinking he was going to tell me something special—like he had bought a present for someone. He moved closer to me. I now had to lie on my back. Daddy was now on his knees—resting on his hands—on all fours over top of me.

"I've made love to every one of your aunts except one," he said. His smile had now gotten broader.

"Uh huh." I answered. My mind began to wander—wondering which of my mother's sisters-in-law my father had not had intercourse with—at the same time—imagining what it must have been like for him to have sex with all those women. Maybe he thought it would turn me on. I've spent years trying to understand what was happening that afternoon. I could smell his cologne—feel his warm breath. He was speaking softly, tenderly. I had spent years—more years than I could remember—wanting my father to love me, but not like this. I was beginning to feel nauseous. I thought I might have to throw up.

"I've had sex with a lot of women," Daddy kept on. "Sometimes women get pregnant. When I was working in Baltimore—now ya mumma doesn't know about this one—I had sex with this woman. She got pregnant. She had a little girl."

I listened as my father continued to speak. As strange and confused as I might have felt at that moment, one thing I know is that he made me feel special, like I was his and his alone. Even if I was being seduced by my father, I was not sure what I should have done. How I should have reacted. I only knew that I was getting the attention from him I had wanted my whole life.

"What happened to the baby?" I asked.

"The mother put her in an orphanage in Baltimore. Some nuns took care of her."

I was wearing shorts. Daddy was wearing khaki pants. I remember his khakis brushing against my bare legs. I remember the thin leather belt and how quickly he could whip it out to swing it at one of us. I remember the beige short-sleeved shirt he was wearing. He was stroking my hair. *Don't move*, I told myself. *Just lie still*.

I looked at the walls and the rose-patterned wallpaper. I looked at the tops of the windows and the dirty white curtains that stretched across them. I looked at the ceiling, the spider-like lines of cracked plaster that ran in every direction across the ceiling. I noticed the chip on the glass of the light fixture above us. I wondered if the light was on. I couldn't remember. It was daylight outside. I looked at my father.

"Jackson, your lunch is ready."

"I'm coming." Daddy laughed.

No matter what happened afterwards, I never really moved past that moment. It was a place where I would always seem to be. On my bed. My father in control of me. He was the man. I wasn't sure what I was. I only knew I had a secret to keep. And in the years that followed, I learned that other children had secrets as well. Things that happened to us. Places where we find ourselves locked inside. Places from which we cannot escape. At least that's what I convinced myself a long time ago. We can keep the secret—or we can speak it and risk having people know the most intimate part of who we are, why we are the way we are. Explaining them does not release their hold on us. It only reveals the depth of our affliction.

As my brothers and I stood in the funeral parlor, I decided to keep my secrets. I would not tell my brothers. I would not talk to the priest.

"Yeah, he's dead," I said as we continued staring at my father's body, "but he's not gone. I'm still afraid of that thing in the coffin. Not because I believe in ghosts, but because he's my father." *And the sins of the father will be visited upon the children for a hundred generations.* I laughed a little. Not too much.

Part Fifteen

Now that the room was empty, I began to hear a sound which had remained constant. In one of the far corners of the parlor, someone—Carter, I supposed— had set up a display, a large digital screen which showed photos taken of my father throughout the years. As some unfamiliar song played softly in the background, one photograph after another faded in and out on the large screen. Some were copies of black and white snapshots taken more than half a century ago. Others were more recent pictures, taken in the hospital just days before he died. What surprised me most about the display, though, was what seemed to be a continued denial, a recusant portrayal of the pain and destruction that was so much a part of my father's reality. As each photo appeared and then dissolved away, a doleful melody struggled to set a mournful mood. Unfortunately, each photograph had its back story.

There were images of Christmases we had celebrated in the white, cement block house, Daddy standing on a ladder stringing colorful lights around the tree. There were pictures of birthday parties held in the backyard, my father managing a little league baseball team—even a photo of Daddy shooting his shotgun in the field behind our house. As mourners looked at the photos—some smiling gently, others visibly amused—I wondered if they knew of the life between the photographs. Did they know how my father would turn violent if the Christmas lights didn't hang just so? Had they seen Daddy's drunken rants as he cursed and swore at unsuspecting visitors after the birthday candles were blown out? Had they heard the vile profanity and threats directed at the neighbors and friends who spent so many hours laboring at the dusty, red-clay field where my brothers once played baseball? Would they still have smiled knowing that the man with the shotgun had nearly beaten to death the small child standing next to him in the photograph?

As a picture of my mother and father standing next to one another with their three sons dissolved on the screen—an image taken in a photo booth at a county fair faded in . . . Daddy smiling brightly with a teenage Jolene held tightly to his chest. Over the course of five minutes or so, dozens of photographs faded in and out of view, as did one dissonant memory after another. Smiling faces tell lies.

The final picture showed my father just a few days prior to his death, an old man with a face that revealed more years than he had lived. The lips that had once pressed hard against the bodies of so many lovers, now curled about gums which held remnants of teeth that had long since rotted away. The nose, once sculpted and well-defined, had now grown narrow and pointed, looking more like a bird's beak. And the eyes which once had the power to pierce into the depths of my soul had now fallen far into their sockets, growing dimmer with each passing moment. My father knew he was dying.

The last time I had seen my father was more than a year before his death. I had stopped to visit him on an infrequent trip to Richmond. The years of cigarettes, rage, and alcohol in its many forms had taken an obvious toll on him. An oxygen cannula ran to his nose. We sat in the same room, about six feet across from each another, speaking only an occasional word or phrase. Talking about the weather, or if he had any aches or pains.

"I'm awright," was his quick-said standard response.

After a number of strokes, heart attacks, surgeries and prostate cancer had left him debilitated, he was now confined to a wheelchair.

"Well, I'm gonna be heading up the road," I said after sitting in rarely-interrupted silence for more than an hour.

"Awright," my father answered. "How about helping me into bed?" My father had never asked me to help him to do anything in any way at any time in my life. I wasn't sure what to say or if I should say anything. For an instant, there was a sense of power.

"Sure," I said.

I pushed him into his bedroom and placed the chair close to the side of the bed.

"I'm so tired," he said.

Leaning over, I placed one arm around my father's chest and, cradling his legs with my other arm, I lifted him from the chair and gently placed him in bed. His body seemed little more than flesh and bones. I guess he weighed about a hundred pounds. He moaned quietly. I could tell he was hurting.

"I love you, Ran," he said as I pulled the blanket to his chest.

"I love you, too, Dad," I answered. He closed his eyes.

I stood staring at my father. For a brief moment, I thought about speaking to him about the secrets I carried about the two of us. But I didn't. There would have been no use, I told myself. Even if we had spoken—if our conversation had lasted long into the night—if we had broached those subjects which had been locked away for decades—it would have done no good. My father did not have the power to undo the things he had done so long ago. The damage had been done. I closed the door. That was the last time I saw my father.

It was late when I finally left the funeral home. Relatives had invited me to spend the night with them, but I preferred a hotel room. I wanted to be alone and, for some reason, being alone in Richmond felt more normal. As the night continued to unfold, I lay in my bed. The night had exhausted me. At some point, after several hours of looking in the darkness, I began listening to the words and phrases of the multitude of conversations I had been a part of since my arrival at the funeral home. While a number of the discussions were the anticipated reliving of the past, the majority of exchanges were narratives of the final months of my father's life. Adult children had spoken to me of how my father had asked for forgiveness, telling of his profound sorrow for the pain he had inflicted. Theresa, one of my father's other children, spoke of how Daddy's heart was obviously broken—not only by the diseases which had taken such a toll on his physical body, but more so by the knowledge of the suffering he had inflicted upon so many for so long. Daughter after daughter, son after son spoke—each as a witness—having seen a man torn apart as the realization of what had been his life had come crashing down upon him . . . a man humbled and ashamed. There's was a father begging for forgiveness and longing for a reconciliation of broken hearts.

"I was setting there next to him," William, another of his other sons explained, "watching him cry. Thinking he was in pain. I told him I would ask the nurse to give him some stronger medicine. But Daddy said, 'No. That's not why I'm crying. I'm so sorry for everything I did to hurt you—for not being there for you as a father should've been. For not protecting you, for not loving you. I'm so sorry.'"

Throughout the night, I kept hearing the words of those stories over and over in my head. I began to wonder if something had changed in my father's life, or was something changing in mine. I also wondered if through some collective gathering of suffering souls, my father's other family was my own as well. Had our experiences created something greater of us that we could ever hope to be as individuals? Each of us, as individuals and as some perversion of a family, had experienced a hollowing-out of our humanity. We had become shadows of people, shells of what we could have become. I wondered if the death of our joy, the cessation of our laughter, the decay of our happiness had in some maddening way created a generation of spiritless beings. Each of us knew that the landscape of our own childhoods was nothing more than a wasteland. Perhaps this journey had created some mystical union between us. In the midst of my father's death, life was changing and I could not understand why. But what if I had been in that room standing next to my father's bed? Would he have asked me for forgiveness as well? Perhaps he *was* sorry. But did he really remember everything he had done?

I began to imagine the conversation.

"I'm sorry, Ran?"

"For what?"

"For everything I did to you."

"What exactly is it you are sorry for?"

"Everything."

"Sorry, old man," I would say, "I'm not going to let you off that easy. Before I forgive you, let me remind you of what you did."

Daddy would be lying there, silent.

"Well, one of the first memories is when I thought you were going to kill us when we were in the car on our way back from the Tyrell's house in Maryland. Remember?"

"No. I'm sorry, I don't."

"Tough shit, Daddy. It still counts even if you don't remember it. And then there was the time when you smashed all of the china in the kitchen."

"Yeah, I'm sorry for that."

"And then there were—hell, Daddy, I don't know how many . . . a hundred, five hundred, a thousand—when you whipped us or played these perverted games . . . ."

My imagining of the conversation continued for much of the night. Somewhere along the way, though, I began to wonder if I wasn't being too hard on my father. Yes, he had done a lot to make my life miserable. In addition to the physical violence and mental anguish, he had also been "missing in action." He had skipped out on every fatherly responsibility—except for providing room and board for the first few years of my life. But did that make him a bad man? He missed my school graduations. He didn't show up at my wedding or even acknowledge the birth of my children. But was he really evil? I began to think about my own fathering—and what my own children would hold me liable for. Had I failed because my parents had failed me—or would I have failed in spite of them, no matter what my childhood would have been like? Would I really have forced my father to accept responsibility for each and every offense? Maybe Carter was right. Maybe it was time to let it go.

As the sun began to show through the curtains of my room, I thought about all of the things I had wanted to tell Father Jenkins. But as I prepared my litany, I wondered if there were things he had already heard, but could not tell me.

He could not tell me what sins my father had confessed to him. He could not tell me how sorry my father was or how broken his spirit might have been. He could not tell me if my father had wept uncontrollably in those first meetings between the two of them—or if he had stared off silently into a life he grieved. He could only admit that they had not talked much about the past—a past filled with the women he had screwed, the children he had fathered, the sons and daughters he had abused and the life he had thrown away, the legacy of suffering he had endowed.

The next morning, I arrived at the funeral home early, sitting with family members in a large room off to the side of the parlor where my father's body lay. I said hello to Father Jenkins—nothing more—and sat next to Carter who was busy fidgeting with papers and notes concerning the order of the funeral service.

As the service started, our family moved into the larger parlor to sit among others who had come to bury my father. We sang a few hymns, and after the priest offered some prayers and blessings, it was time for the sharing of any remembrances. Carter walked to the front of the room, unfolded a paper and spoke about our father's achievements. He recalled his involvement in unions and clubs, his commitment to his work and his acceptance of black people. Jack and I sat among my father's other children. Some smiled; others sat stone-faced—and occasionally someone wept.

After a prayer at the grave, we each said our goodbyes. Funerals are always filled with suggestions of getting together again, or not waiting until another funeral before seeing one another—but usually that's as far as the conversation goes. Nothing ever happens after that. No matter how well intentioned, we would each go our own way. And we would carry with us the memories we wished we didn't have. After family members, friends and acquaintances had left, I stood and looked at the scores of granite slabs which covered the hillside. Grave markers inscribed with the names of others who have lived and died. I imagined the children who had brought their parents to this place. I thought of the children who wished they had known their parents under different circumstances. I thought of the children who wished they had not known their parents at all. That was me. I looked at my daddy's casket, still hovering over the hole that had been dug for him. A couple of colored-men (as Daddy would have said) stood nearby, smoking cigarettes while I took my time standing at the graveside. I walked over to the heap of flowers covering my father's casket and plucked a small blossom. I tucked it in the pocket of my sport coat.

Part Sixteen

"That's my story." I sat back on the couch, exhausted from the ordeal of giving voice to all of the things which had been hidden away for so very long. "Yeah, it took me a few sessions to get it all out, but now you know it all." The room was quiet. "So when do I get out of here?"

"Obviously, that's not your entire story," the man responded, "or you wouldn't be here."

"Yeah, whatever."

"What does that mean?" he asked.

"It means fuck you."

"And what does that mean?" he continued.

"We both know why I'm here," I said.

"And why is that?"

"Shit, you mean I have to say it?"

"It's important that you own your actions—that you understand the reality of what you did."

"Ok. I thought about killing myself."

"Thought about it?" the man asked. "If you had just thought about it, you wouldn't be here."

"Hard ass, aren't you?" I answered. "Ok. I tried to kill myself."

"What did you do?"

"You want details?" I was losing my patience.

"Yes."

For a moment, I didn't say anything. I just stared at the man sitting across from me in his white hospital coat. He was older than me. That was good because I didn't trust anyone who was younger than me. The top of his head was bald while the sides were covered with white, bushy hair. "Alfred Schonbaum, M.D." was embroidered just above the left chest pocket. There was a stethoscope tucked into his side pocket. Since he was a psychiatrist, it didn't make sense to me why he carried one. *Did he listen to people's heads?* I wanted to crack a joke, but I thought the humor would have been lost on him.

"Ok," I said. I took a deep breath. "I went to the office I had in my house and sat down at my desk. Then I pulled out a sheet of paper and wrote a long note to my children. I explained that I loved them very much, but that I just couldn't go on living. I had had enough. It took me a while to write it. I was crying the whole time; my eyes had become so swollen that I couldn't see what I was writing."

"What did you write?"

"I told them I just couldn't live anymore. My kids aren't dumb. They knew the pain I was in . . . how much I struggled to get past the shit of my life. At least I think they knew."

"Anyway, after that I went to the storage room in our basement, a place where there were metal beams running across the ceiling. I rummaged through the power tools in there and found one of those heavy-duty extension cords, one of the ones I used to do yard work—you know, the big orange ones."

Dr. Schonbaum jotted down notes as I spoke, occasionally glancing over the glasses that sat on the end of his nose.

"There was also an empty bucket in there, a big one made out of molded plastic. I turned it upside down and stood on it. Then I took the electric cord and wrapped it around one of the metal beams a few times. I pulled on it real hard to make sure it wouldn't break—that it would hold my weight. I mean, if I was going to hang myself, I didn't want to screw it up. I wanted to make sure the cord wasn't going to snap. Shit, it would've been pretty awful if I had just broken my neck and not killed myself. I didn't want to end up being paralyzed and not dead."

The doctor continued writing, still not saying a word.

"Once I was sure the cord was going to hold me, I made a loop with a knot and put the cord around my neck. I pulled it taut and then made the length of cord between the beam and my neck tight."

"After that, I took a deep breath. I really don't know why—to relax myself, I suppose. Kind of stupid since the whole idea of hanging yourself is to empty the body of air, not fill it. Anyway, when I was sliding my feet to the outer edge of the bucket so that I could push off and drop, the damnedest thing happened. While I was moving my feet, the bucket started to shift. I almost fell off of it. I thought, shit, I'm going to die before I can kill myself." I laughed. The doctor didn't.

"Well, I got so scared that I pulled the cord off my neck, got down, and ran outside. I called my brother, Jack, and told him what happened. Now, I'm here."

"Was that the first time you'd tried to kill yourself?" Schonbaum asked.

"Well, it was the first time I had gone that far."

"So you've gotten further along each time."

"Yeah, I guess."

He wrote more.

"I've seen people who've killed themselves so I know what's coming," I continued. "I know what it looks like—what they looked like. The eyes fill with blood. The face, hands, feet all turn black. Vomit—even blood—sometimes ooze out of the mouth, maybe out of the nose, even the ears. Sometimes people change their minds halfway into it. I've seen it."

"Anyone you knew?" he asked.

"No, they were strangers. Just bodies. My last year in college, I worked for an ambulance company in Richmond. Those were the days before EMTs or paramedics. A company would just hire you, give you advanced first aid training and then put you in an ambulance made from a cargo van. Not much more than a box van with a red light on top. Boy, I could tell you some shit."

"There was this one time," I continued, "when this guy had set the table in his dining room with nice dishes and silverware. There was a lace tablecloth, fringe all around the bottom. He had also cooked all this food—ham biscuits, potato salad—even fried chicken. Quite a spread. After he had fixed the nice dinner, he'd sat down at the head of the table, put a shotgun in his mouth, and pulled the trigger. His brains were sprayed all over the wall behind him. It was crazy. What made it even more bizarre was that one of the guys who had been called to help clean up the mess had decided to eat some of the ham biscuits while he scraped the dead guy's brains off the wall. Death is a strange, awesome thing."

"Another time, we were called to come get the body of a high school kid who had gone out to hang himself in the woods near his house. It was out in Mechanicsville, where I grew up, but I didn't know him. He had gone about fifty yards into the woods. By the time our ambulance got there, the police had already cut him down from a tree. I picked him up under the arms and my partner grabbed the feet. We put him in a body bag and then onto a reeves stretcher. I'll never forget it; he had deep claw marks on his neck. Evidently, he had dug his fingers in trying to get the rope from around his neck while he was still hanging. He had changed his mind. Poor kid."

"So you've put a lot of thought into this?"

"Yeah."

"Did you think about who would find you after you were dead?" He stopped writing, put his pen in his pocket, and looked at me.

"Not really."

"People rarely do," he said. "so it could have been one of your kids—even your youngest. Do you think that would be something they could ever forget?"

I had to admit, I hadn't really thought about my children. I had only wanted to find some way to get out of the pain I was in. But Schonbaum's words made me think about each of them—one by one. I envisioned their faces. Their voices. I imagined the tears they would have cried, for weeks, months, years. I didn't respond.

"So what will stop you from going through with it the next time?" he continued.

"I don't know."

The room was silent again.

"With all that you have been through—the extreme inappropriateness . . . or let's just call it molestation by your father . . . because in essence, whether he physically had sex with you or not, that's what it was: molestation; the seduction by your mother . . . ." He flipped the pages of his notebook back from one page to another as he continued to speak. "Seeing your brother get beaten repeatedly—

almost to the point of death—the violence continually perpetrated by your father, the death of animals . . . with all that you've been through, I'm surprised you're not a serial killer."

I laughed loudly. He didn't.

"Have you ever killed anyone?"

"No."

"Have you ever thought about killing anyone?"

"Yeah. Myself."

"Anyone else?"

"I've mostly spent my adult life wishing I had never been born," I explained. "But I was born. And now, I am here in this place. I have to deal with it."

"How are you feeling right now?" he asked.

"Pretty groggy."

"That's the medication. It should level out in the next day or two. You will need to stay on medication for a while. Will you commit to that?"

"Sure," I said. While I would have said anything he wanted to hear in order to get out of the psych unit, I was telling the truth. I was tired of being where I was—the hellhole that had become my life. Eating myself into a grave. The constant despair. Crying incessantly.

"Do you know what day this is?" the doctor asked still writing on his pad.

"Yeah, don't you?" I said trying to find humor. "It's Tuesday—maybe Wednesday."

"It's Tuesday," he laughed. "I'll be back tomorrow afternoon. We can talk some more. I want to see how you're doing in twenty-four hours."

"Lovely. Fuck you very much." I laughed. He looked at me.

"What does that mean?" he said without smiling.

"I don't know," I answered. "What am I supposed to say? Thank you? Get real. It means that I'm tired of all this shit—the anxiety, the pain, the depression, living a shell of a life. Look, as hard as it may be to believe, I'm actually a pretty religious guy. I usually don't curse or swear—at least I try not to. But I've had it with life, so anything and anyone are fair game. I just want out."

"Ok," he said again, "we'll talk more tomorrow. Have a good evening." With that, he stood up and opened the door to let me out of the conference room. I walked back to my room and lay in bed.

The next morning was the same as those of the previous week had been. Up by 8:00. Scrambled eggs, orange or apple juice, cold cereal and a tiny carton of milk. Plastic sporks and paper napkins. Each morning, I scooped up a sporkful of eggs. I looked at them intently, examining their color. How yellow should they have been? Were they too yellow? I sniffed them—first with one nostril, then the other. Moving them back and forth under my nose, I tried to detect even the slightest hint of the smell of fish. I laughed. A little.

In a lot of ways, except for their name, psychiatric hospitals haven't changed a lot since the time when my mother was in one more than forty years earlier. Even though the facilities are now called "Behavioral Health Units," there were still metal grates over the windows and locks on all the doors. Security cameras were everywhere. There were no cords on the phones. No belts to hold a person's pants up. No shoe laces. No electrical outlets. No glass that could have been broken or used. No protruding light fixtures to tie a rope to. No shower heads, towel bars, or curtain rods to have hung from. No privacy. And when we weren't talking to a doctor, in group therapy, making a craft, or watching television, nearly everyone slept—or cried. I did a lot of both.

One man, I never really got to know his name, spent a lot of time talking to his left sneaker. Even during meals, he would look down at his shoe, ask it if it wanted to come up, then take it off and hold it at eye-level. He would mumble through a conversation with the shoe. Talking baby-talk. He would laugh, sometimes giggle. I don't know if he had the same relationship with his wing tips, but the sneaker was definitely very special to him.

Another guy—Larry—talked to people that none of us could see. I'm not going to say that Larry was delusional, because maybe the person he was talking to was really there. Perhaps I was the delusional one. Maybe I just couldn't see what was really there. People do that, you know—struggle with the ability to see and appreciate the beauty and value of something that is right there in front of them. Whatever. Larry cried sometimes. I never asked him why.

Brenda, a petite woman who probably weighed little more than a hundred pounds, cried incessantly. Sobbing, weeping, moaning. It happens. We each

have our own problems. Candace, a young woman in
her early thirties, spent most of her time talking about
sex—whom she had had sex with, what kind it was,
where they did it, what it was like, if she had an
orgasm or not. Those of us who heard her were never
aroused by the stories. Our reaction was more often
curiosity as to why she had screwed some guy she had
just met in a laundromat in the middle of the day.

Altogether, there were about twenty of us in the
unit—men and women, young and not so young.
Black, white, Hispanic and Asian. We all had our
demons, back-stories, addictions, issues, and baggage.
And then there was Allison.

An overweight, middle-aged lady, I guess you
could say that Allison and I became somewhat-
kindred spirits. She had dark brown hair and skin that
had been ravaged by acne. She was also bi-polar,
severely depressed, and prone to panic attacks. At
least, that's what she told me. Her husband, Paul,
came to visit her every evening right after supper. He
always brought with him a fresh batch of pictures
from their children. Colored drawings that said
something like "Mommy, come home soon!" or "We
love you." After Paul left, Allison would cry for about
an hour.

"I don't want to be here," she would say in the
midst of the tears, "but I don't want to kill myself
either."

"I hear you," was my standard response.

"Some people want to be here," she told me.
"Some people like it here because they feel safe—like

no one can harm them here and that they can't harm themselves." "Harming one's self" was professional jargon for suicide.

"I had decided to kill myself and my children," Allison continued. "I know that's not right, but it made sense to me. I mean, why would they want to live if I wasn't going to be around?" I never really answered her questions. That wasn't why she was talking. That wasn't why any of us spoke. The only reason we talked was to get the questions, thoughts, or stories out of our heads. The doctor was the one who was in charge of giving us answers. I listened to Allison's questions and she listened to mine.

"This isn't supposed to be my life," I said when it was my turn to talk. "I had a wonderful wife, great kids, a house, a job, a nice life. People would have died for what I had. But I never could see that. For my whole fucking life . . . ." I stopped for a moment. "I'm sorry, do you mind if I say fucking?"

"I don't mind," Allison laughed. "I'm a Christian, so I don't use those words, but I don't get offended if someone else does."

I began laughing, too, caught up in the irony of our conversation. *At some point, she had rationalized that it was okay to kill her family and be a Christian, but she couldn't rationalize that it was okay for a Christian to say "fuck."*

"Okay, thanks," I continued. "Anyway, I've spent my whole life caught up in where I came from—who my parents were, how screwed up they were, and how screwed up I am because of everything I went through as a kid. For my whole fucking life, I've let everything that I experienced growing up define me." I ranted for a while longer—describing the unfairness and horror of my childhood. When there was a moment of silence, Allison spoke.

"Your kids, do they love you?" she asked.

"What?" I responded. In a lot of ways, she was breaking the rules—asking me a question about something I had just told her. But I didn't mind.

"Yes, they do. Since I've been in here, they've all called me . . . wanting to know what they can do to help. They want me to know that they love me and care about me."

"Sounds like you've got something to live for." We were quiet for a moment. The activities room where we sat had emptied after Candace had finished another one of her sex stories. Allison spoke freely.

"You've got a life to live," Allison continued. "After you get out of here, it's up to you to choose how you are going to live it. You can choose to be the person who lets himself be defined by his childhood or you can be the person who decides how he will be defined."

"Easier said than done."

"Of course it is," she responded. "That's why there are meds to get us through this. But they don't have to define who we are and they don't have to be forever."

"So much wisdom!" I mocked.

"I've been down this road a lot," Allison continued. "And when I'm not in here, I'm a therapist with my own patients."

I laughed a little. "Ah," I said. "You're one of the 'walking wounded,'" a term used to refer to people who had become therapists after having experienced their own trauma. "So are you saying this for my benefit or for your own?" I asked.

"Both." She smiled. "Ok, whatever I do," she said rephrasing her words, "I have to remember that when I choose how I am going to live, I am also choosing what kind of legacy I will leave—what kind of gift I will give my children to carry with them and pass along to their children as well. My parents gave me a legacy. A really crappy one. But that doesn't have to be what I pass along to my children. I can choose something different. Something better. Laying in my bathtub with my veins open and watching the blood wash down the drain sure is different, but it isn't better."

Neither of us said anything after that. The suicide factor had sobered our conversation. I headed for my room to take a nap.

"James," a young nurse said standing in the doorway of my room. I hated it when people called me that. "Are you awake?"

"Sure," I answered.

"Dr. Schonbaum is in the conference room. He wants to see you."

I didn't want to get up. I wanted to sleep. Most of all, though, I didn't want to talk about the past anymore. I didn't want to think about it or even consider it. It was over—and it had been for decades.

"How are you feeling today?" the doctor asked as I walked into the conference room. "Were you asleep?"

"I'm okay," I answered. "Yeah."

"So tell me about what you are thinking today. Are you still wanting to harm yourself?"

"Honestly?" I asked.

"Yes. Please."

"Well," I paused. "No."

"What has changed?"

"I've been doing a lot of thinking," I said. "I've come to the realization that if I killed myself, I wouldn't be giving my kids much of a going away present. I mean, they would be getting a pretty shitty gift from me—something that would tear them apart for the rest of their lives."

"Remember the friend I talked about a while ago? My friend, Jeff Carpenter?" I continued talking without giving him a chance to answer. "Jeff was a great kid—funny, smart, good with girls—they loved him—fun to be with. I could go on for a while. I could probably also tell you a half-dozen stories about things we did together . . . hunting, fishing, Boy Scouts, school. But you know what I remember about him most? The fact that he blew his brains out. Sad, isn't it? People can do all kinds of great things in their lives—be great people, great friends, great brothers, sisters, parents. Hell, even be a great president. But when someone dies a horrible death, that's what we remember about them most. I guess you could say that if I killed myself, I would be doing to my kids something just as bad—if not worse—than what my parents did to me. I don't want to be responsible for that."

Instead of writing on his pad, Dr. Schonbaum was staring straight at me. "That's good. Sounds like the medication is working."

"I guess so," I answered.

"Anything else?" he asked.

As I sat there, I thought about any number of things I could have said to him. I could have continued my rant from our previous sessions— explaining to him how I had survived my father's brutality. *People aren't just supposed to spend their lives mearly surviving. People are supposed to thrive. Surviving is what people do when they are just clinging to life.*

Yeah, I was working on giving Schonbaum the right answers, but it would take me a while before I could believe that I had something to be thankful for or worth living for. *I didn't have scars on my face from my father punching me. I got smacked around a lot, but no punches to the face. Jack couldn't make that statement. I didn't get whipped until I nearly bled to death. Yeah, I was whipped. With a belt, a wooden paddle, a switch, broad smacks with an open hand. Sometimes even a rap of the knuckles across the mouth. But Jack got worse ones. I never lost any blood; Jack did—lots of it. And I didn't get sodomized by perverted kids in Boy Scouts. They almost pulled it off, but not quite—I survived that, too. I didn't blow my head off like some of my friends had. I didn't kill anybody else either. Would it have been better— wouldn't there have been a lot less pain—if I would've died an early death like my friend Jeff? Are Carter and Jack better men, too, for surviving?*

Looking back, I wish I hadn't gone through any of it. I would rather not have memories of killing animals—even those whimpering at the bottom of a pit. I would be content not knowing how to reconnect the electricity or water after one or the other or both had been shut off for non-payment. I would prefer not to know about women being murdered by their husbands. If by not going through any of it I would be a little less wise, that would be fine. If having different parents would have made me a bit weaker when difficult circumstances arise, that would have been fine, too. I could always call my parish priest or some other professional do-gooder. That would be okay. Weak is okay.

I wish I didn't have secrets—about my father's insatiable perversion. About my mother's silent seduction. About Boy Scouts determined to abuse one of their own. I'm sure my brothers have their own secrets. Everyone has secrets. My father's other children have them as well. I know Thomas does.

I wanted to tell the doctor how the insight about the legacy parents leave their children had come to me from another patient, a woman who had gained wisdom from her own suffering. I wanted to dispute the impact a few pills were having on me. Okay, maybe the meds were working. The biggest impact, though, seemed to be coming from seeing other people living shells of their lives—shadows of who they were meant to be. A man having lunch with his sneaker; a woman telling tales about her sex life; a man talking to an invisible friend; a woman who cried for a week. It was time for me to thrive—to leave my addictions behind. It was time for me to leave my childhood and all of the pain and poison of its memories. It was time for me to be the man I was created to be, not the one I had become—a man who tried to control or manipulate anything and everything in his life out of fear that he might become his father. In the end, why I had changed didn't really seem to matter. The doctor's job was done. I wasn't choosing suicide anymore.

"I'm good," I said. Dr. Schonbaum smiled.

A few months later, on a Saturday, Jack and I met at Holy Cross Cemetery in Richmond's north side. Carter was busy with work—even on a Saturday. We had thought about rescheduling, trying to set a time when the three of us could be together. But it was August 17. Whoever could make it would be there.

Jack had driven up from Louisiana earlier in the week. He was spending time visiting his daughter, Rebecca, who had just given birth to her first child—ck's first grandchild. I had driven down from Pennsylvania the night before and stayed at a motel just outside of Richmond. It was noon when I pulled into the cemetery. Jack was already standing on the grass next to our father's grave.

"Hey," he said as I got out of my car.

"Hey, bro," We gave each other a kiss on the cheek and hugged for a moment. "Been here long?" I asked.

"Just a few minutes. I was just talking to the old man while I was waiting."

"Oh yeah?" I asked. "Did he have anything to say?"

"Nah. 'Course, he never was much on conversation." We both laughed. "How you been?"

"Awright," I said. "Good to be on the outside and working again."

"How's your love life?"

"What love life?" I laughed. "I know. You wouldn't know what that's like. You've been screwing anything that walks since you were thirteen."

"Not true."

"What?" I could not believe what I was hearing. My middle brother's sexual prowess and long list of female conquests had been the conversation of family gatherings for decades.

"You know the first time I had sex?" Jack asked. My brother was somewhat serious now. He looked at me in a way I had not seen in a long time.

"Yeah, I've heard the story. You and Cathy Turner—the two of you were in that old barn. You were thirteen and she was what—fourteen, fifteen?"

"That's what everybody thought," he explained. "I only made it to second base with her, no home run. But I wasn't going to tell anybody anything different. She and I got into that barn and started making out. Only thing was I didn't know what to do. Kissing and getting my hand under her shirt was the most I had ever done. Hell, even Daddy tried to get me laid."

"Are you kiddin' me?"

As we stood beside our father's grave, Jack shared a story he had long held to himself. The time when he had accompanied our father on one of Daddy's Saturday afternoon drives to Spotsylvania to see Jolene.

The Dotsons' farm was an old, rundown clapboard house that had once been white. It had a faded tin roof and a rotting wooden porch that jutted out from the front. The porch then wrapped around to the side all the way to the back door. It wasn't a large house, three bedrooms at the most. The old place sat in the middle of a stand of tall oaks and maples. There was an open field to the left. They grew corn, some tomatoes, peppers, pole beans and cabbage as the seasons allowed. After our parents had separated, it was the place where Daddy spent most every weekend.

My father's Pontiac made its way slowly up to the house. There wasn't much of a driveway—just lots of sandy dirt with chickens running close to the house and under the porch. This particular afternoon when Daddy and Jack arrived, Jolene's daddy— Billy—her two uncles, and her older brother were sitting on the porch. Some were in chairs. Others sat on the floor with their backs against the wall. They had been drinking most of the day.

"I told them I was bringing you with me," Daddy explained to Jack as the car made its way through the trees and closer to the house. Some of Jolene's family is gonna be there and she's got a cousin you might like. Pinky. Pretty little thing."

"Hey, Dick," Jolene's father called out as we made our way to the porch. Dick. That was the name Daddy had chosen to be known by whenever he was away from his real family. It seemed appropriate.

"Hey, Billy," Daddy answered. "You boys started without me."

"Well, we knew you'd be here sooner or later. You'll just have to drink a bit faster to catch up." They laughed. "Who ya got with you?"

"This is my boy, Jack."

"Hey, Jack," Billy Dotson yelled.

"Hey," Jack answered.

"Where are the girls?" Daddy shouted, still walking toward the house.

"They're out back in the kitchen," Billy said. "Damn, you're anxious!" All of the men on the porch laughed.

"I want Jack to meet Pinky."

"Yeah, she's anxious to meet him, too. That's all she's talked about all morning, 'Dick's son is coming. I wonder what he looks like. Do you think he's cute?'" The laughter continued.

"Pinky," Billy Dotson finally yelled. "Pinky! Dick's here and he brought somebody with him."

An old screen door could be heard slamming shut somewhere in the back. A pretty girl, about thirteen years old with short blonde hair came running around the corner of the house. Breathless, she stood pushing her hair behind her ears.

"Pinky, this is my son Jack," Daddy said.

The two smiled at each other. "Hi," they each said taking turns.

To a lot of people it wouldn't make sense why a father would hand his teenage daughter over to have sex with a boy—any boy. Much less a boy he didn't even know. But at that place, at that time, it really wasn't strange at all. The Dotson men knew my daddy. They knew he had fathered Jolene's child and they knew that after she became pregnant, he had not shirked his responsibilities—at least not after the "insurance man" had found out where Daddy lived. Daddy had taken care of them financially. To those men sitting on the porch that afternoon, Jack was a safe bet. They knew their daughters were going to lose their virginity. So why not by a boy who came from "good stock?" Daddy had taken care of Jolene. And if Pinky became pregnant, Jack would take care of her.

Still standing in the dirt in front of the house, Daddy turned away from the others and faced my brother. He handed Jack the keys to the Pontiac. "Here," he said. "You and Pinky go on down to that building down the road where I used to work. You remember where it is, don't you?" Jack nodded. "Go make yourself a man."

My brother and I stood at the edge of our father's grave.

"So what happened?" I asked.

"Nothing. I had no idea what to do. Pinky and I drove down to the old place where Daddy used to work, but all we did was sit in the car and make out. I think I felt her up a little. After all the stories of me with girls and stuff, people might not believe it, but the first time I had sex was with a hooker when I was in the Navy—in '72, I think. It was in the Philippines. It cost me five dollars. But what I learned from Daddy was that the only thing women were good for was having babies. That's why he left Mumma. When she couldn't have babies anymore, she was worthless."

We both stood there still staring at the grave. The sun was hot. The only sound was that of a car occasionally passing by the other side of the cemetery wall.

"Did you hear what somebody wanted to put on the headstone?" I asked.

"What?"

"Devoted father." We both laughed.

"Different people have different memories," he said.

"And some people are nuts."

My brother and I had put our arms around each other's shoulders. We stared at the granite headstone that bore Daddy's name.

"You and Carter and me—we've done okay," he said. "We've got good kids. We provided for them. Gave them a roof over their heads. Food to eat. Clothes. They went to school, college. They never wanted for anything. Yeah, shit happens. Marriages fall apart, but that happens to everybody." My brother drew heavy from cigarette.

"We did okay," he continued. "We went through a lot, but it made us stronger because of it. We survived. Think about it, Randy," he concluded. "We're better men because of it."

"Maybe," I said, "These days, though, I'm thinking that I'm a good man in spite of what we went through, not because of it. And, unlike Daddy, I think our kids will remember us for how much we loved them—not how much we beat them."

We both stood staring at the headstone for a moment, then walked back to our cars. We planned to find a place nearby to have lunch.

"I'm starving," I said. "Where we going to eat?"

"I don't know," he replied. "But first I need to stop someplace where I can find a bottle of vodka. I'm empty."

CPSIA information can be obtained
at www.ICGtesting.com
Printed in the USA
BVOW08s0431120118
505106BV00001B/37/P